Name _____

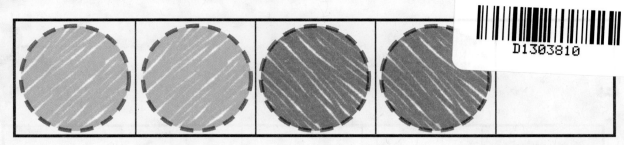

minus

4 --- _____   _____

- -

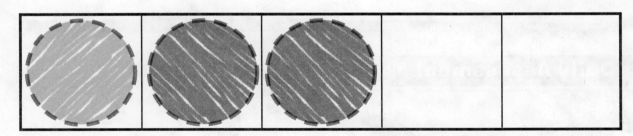

minus

3 --- _____   _____

DIRECTIONS **3.** Place 4 counters in the five frame. Trace the counters. Write the number of counters that are red. Write the number of counters that are yellow. Trace the symbol. **4.** Place 3 counters in the five frame. Trace the counters. Write the number of counters that are red. Write the number of counters that are yellow. Trace the symbol.

HOME ACTIVITY • Show your child a set of 5 small objects. Take away three objects. Have him or her describe how you decomposed the set.

Problem Solving

5

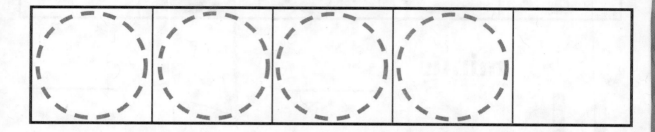

Daily Assessment Task

6

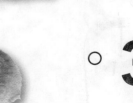

○ **2**

○ **3**

DIRECTIONS **5.** There are 4 counters in the five frame. One counter is yellow. How many counters are red? Color the counters. Write the number of counters in the five frame. Write the number of counters that are yellow. Write the number of counters that are red. **6.** Choose the correct answer. There are 4 rabbits. Two of the rabbits are big. How many rabbits are small?

318 three hundred eighteen

TEKS **Number and Operations—K.2.I**
MATHEMATICAL PROCESSES **K.1.C**

9.3
HANDS ON

Decompose Numbers Up to 5

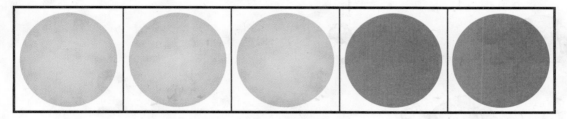

minus

5 --- _____   _____

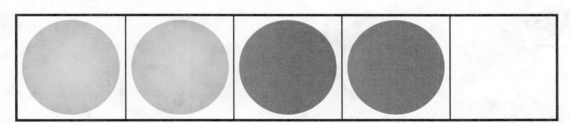

minus

4 --- _____   _____

DIRECTIONS **1.** There are 5 counters in the five frame. Trace the symbol and write the number of counters that are red. Write the number of counters that are yellow. **2.** There are 4 counters in the five frame. Trace the symbol and write the number of counters that are red. Write the number of counters that are yellow.

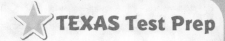

 3

○ **3**

● **2**

4

 1

○ **3**

DIRECTIONS Choose the correct answer. **3.** There are 5 turtles. Three of the turtles are green. How many turtles are brown? **4.** There are 3 rabbits. Two of the rabbits are brown. How many rabbits are white?

TEKS Number and Operations—K.2.I

MATHEMATICAL PROCESSES
K.1.B

9.4
HANDS ON

PROBLEM SOLVING • Compose and Decompose Numbers Up to 5

Essential Question

How can you solve problems using the strategy make a model?

🔑 **Unlock the Problem** Real World

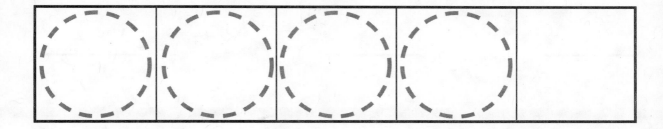

DIRECTIONS Hannah has 4 counters. How many red and yellow counters could she have? Place the red counters in the five frame. Trace and color them. Write the number. Trace the plus symbol. Place the yellow counters in the five frame. Trace and color them. Write the number. Write the number to show how many counters in all.

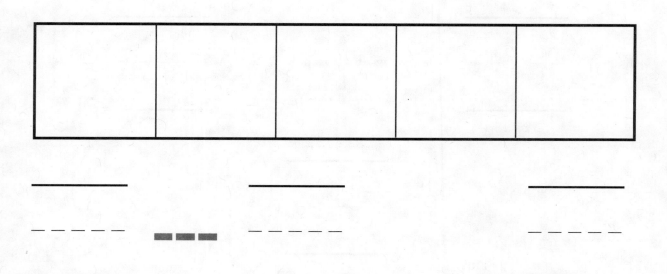

DIRECTIONS **I–2**. Listen to the problem. Draw and color counters to solve the problem. Write the numbers and trace the symbol.

322 three hundred twenty-two

Name _____

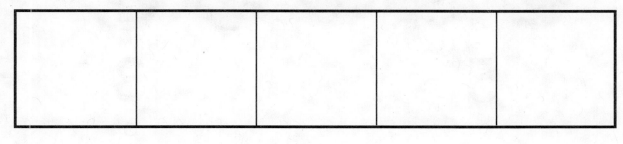

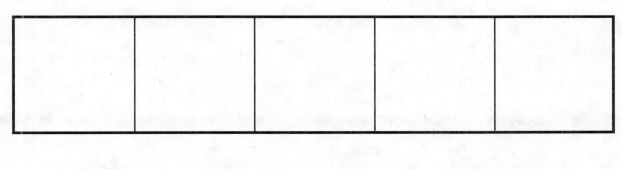

DIRECTIONS **3–4.** Listen to the problem. Draw and color counters to solve the problem. Write the numbers and trace the symbol.

HOME ACTIVITY • Have your child tell a short word problem about one of the pictures on this page.

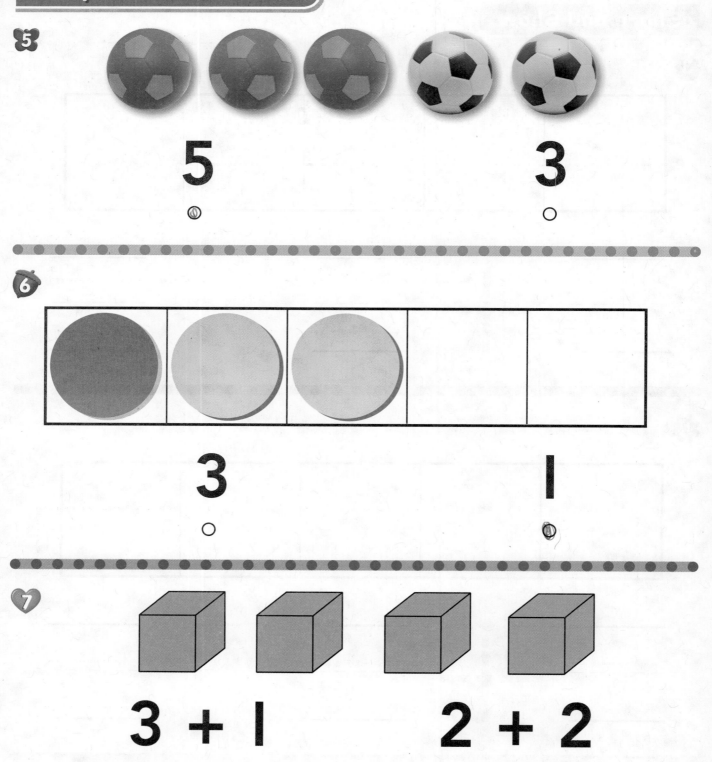

5

5 ○ **3** ○

6

3 ○ **1** ○

7

3 + 1 ○ **2 + 2** ○

DIRECTIONS Listen to the problem. Choose the correct answer. **5.** The soccer team has 3 blue soccer balls. It also has 2 yellow soccer balls. How many soccer balls are there in all? **6.** There are 3 counters. 2 are yellow. The rest are red. How many counters are red? **7.** Which math statement describes the cubes?

TEKS Number and Operations—K.2.I
MATHEMATICAL PROCESSES K.1.B

Name _____

9.4
HANDS ON

PROBLEM SOLVING • Compose and Decompose Numbers Up to 5

1

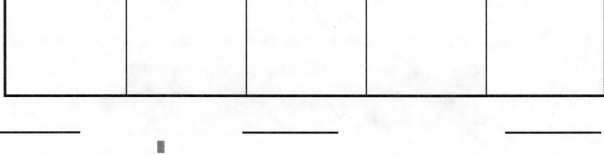

2

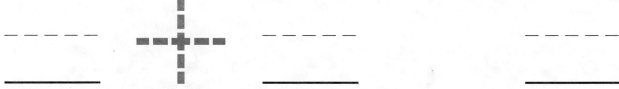

DIRECTIONS 1–2. Draw 5 counters. Color some of them yellow. Write the number. Trace the symbol. Color the rest of the counters red. Write the number. Write the number to show how many counters in all.

 3

○ **5**   ○ **4**

 4

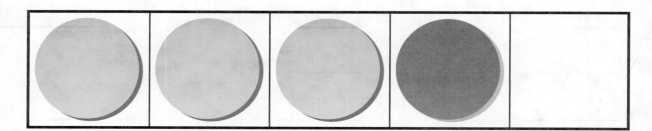

○ **3**   ○ **4**

5

○ **2 + 1**   ○ **3 + 2**

DIRECTIONS Choose the correct answer. **3.** Dean has 2 yellow hats. He also has two purple hats. How many hats does he have in all? **4.** There are 4 counters. 1 is red. The rest are yellow. How many counters are yellow? **5.** Which math statement describes the cubes?

Module 9 Assessment

Concepts and Skills

1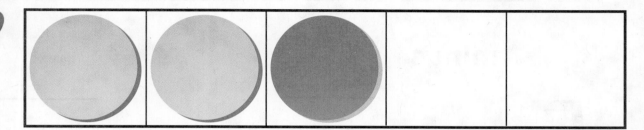

3 _____ and _____

2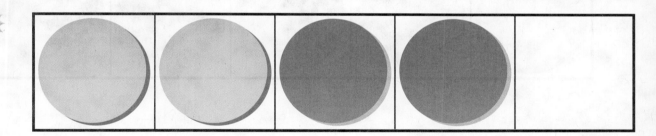

plus

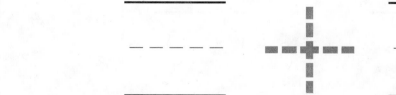

DIRECTIONS **I.** There are 3 counters. Write the number of yellow counters. Write the number of red counters. ✦ TEKS K.2.I **2.** Write the number of counters in all. Write the number of yellow counters. Write the number of red counters. ✦ TEKS K.2.I

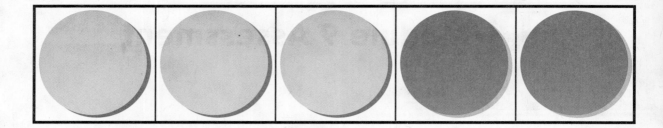

minus

5 -- _____   _____

⭐ **TEXAS Test Prep**

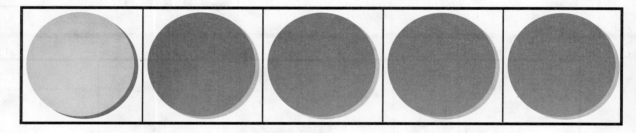

_____   _____   _____

--- ---

_____   _____   _____

DIRECTIONS **3.** Count the counters in the five frame. Write the number of red counters. Trace the symbol. Write the number of yellow counters. ➤ TEKS K.2.I
4. Leila has 5 counters. She has 4 red counters. The rest are yellow. How many yellow counters does Leila have? Write the numbers and trace the symbol. ➤ TEKS K.2.I

TEKS Number and Operations—**K.2.I**
Also K.2.B, K.2.C, K.2.D

MATHEMATICAL PROCESSES
K.1.D, K.1.E

10.1 HANDS ON Compose 6 and 7

? **Essential Question**

How do you put together numbers to make 6 and 7?

Explore

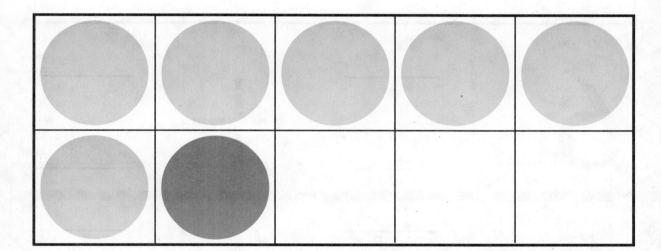

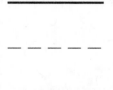

7   _____  _____

DIRECTIONS Place yellow and red counters in the ten frame as shown. Write the numbers and trace the symbol to show the sets that are put together.

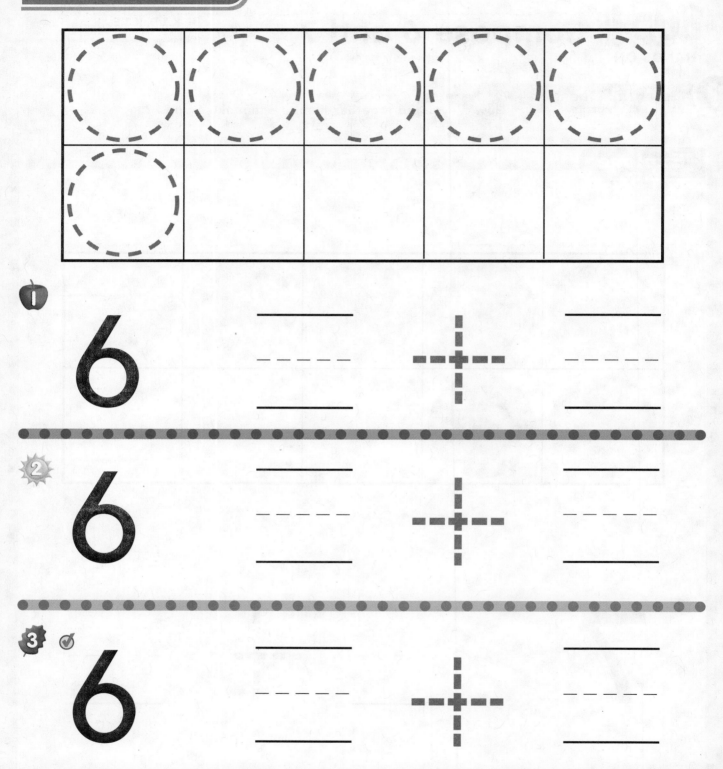

1 6 _ _ _ _ + _ _ _ _

2 6 _ _ _ _ + _ _ _ _

3 ✓ 6 _ _ _ _ + _ _ _ _

DIRECTIONS 1–2. Place counters in the ten frame to model numbers put together to make 6. How many are there of each color counter? Write the numbers and trace the symbol. **3.** Place counters in the ten frame to model numbers put together to make 6. Write the numbers for each color and trace the symbol. Draw and color the counters to match the numbers.

330 three hundred thirty

Name _____

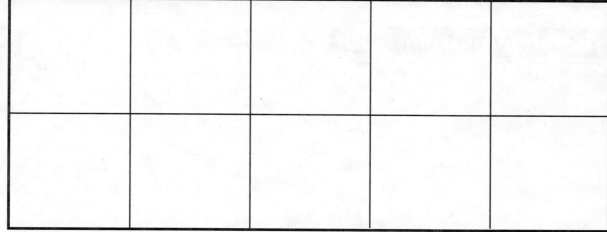

4 7 _____ + _____

5 7 _____ + _____

6 7 _____ + _____

DIRECTIONS **4–5.** Place counters in the ten frame to model numbers put together to make 7. Write the numbers and trace the symbol. **6.** Draw and color counters to model numbers put together to make 7. Write the numbers and trace the symbol.

 HOME ACTIVITY • Show your child a number from 1 to 7. Ask him or her to find the number that makes 6 or 7 when put together with that number.

Problem Solving

7

_____   _____   +   _____
- - - - -   - - - - -   - - - - -
_____   _____   _____

Daily Assessment Task

8

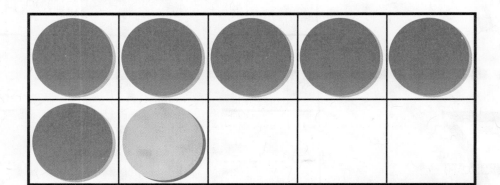

○ **7 + 3**   ○ **6 + 1**

DIRECTIONS **7.** Troy has some toy trucks. Two of the trucks are red. Write the number and trace the symbol. Four of the trucks are blue. Write the number. How many trucks does he have? Draw to solve the problem. Write the number. **8.** Choose the correct answer. Count the counters. Which numbers are put together?

TEKS Number and Operations—K.2.I
Also K.2.B, K.2.C, K.2.D
MATHEMATICAL PROCESSES K.1.D

10.1 HANDS ON Compose 6 and 7

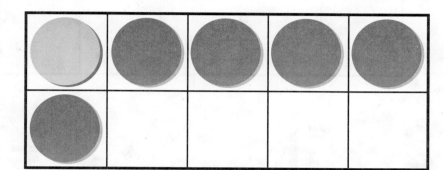

6   _____  _____

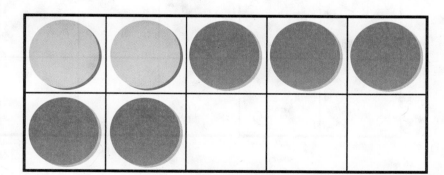

7   _____ + _____

DIRECTIONS 1–2. Count the counters in the ten frame that model numbers put together. How many are there of each color counter? Write the numbers and trace the symbol.

3

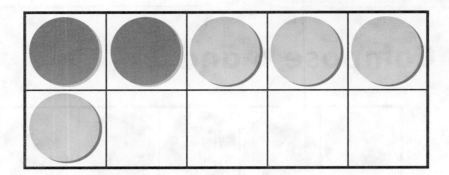

○ $2 + 4$ ● $3 + 3$

4

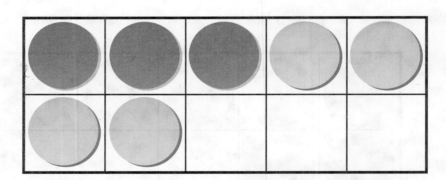

○ $3 + 2$ ● $3 + 4$

DIRECTIONS Choose the correct answer.
3–4. Count the counters. Which numbers are put together?

TEKS **Number and Operations—K.2.I**
Also K.2.B, K.2.C, K.2.D
MATHEMATICAL PROCESSES
K.1.C, K.1.E

10.2
HANDS ON **Compose 8**

? Essential Question

How do you put together numbers to make 8?

Explore

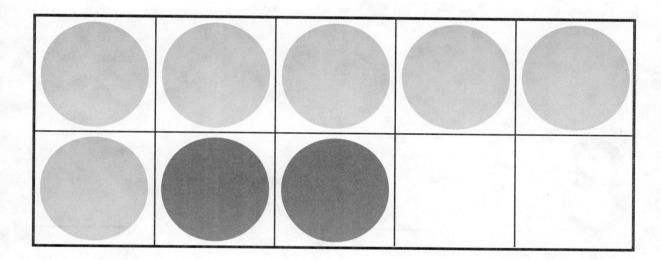

8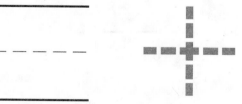

DIRECTIONS Place yellow and red counters in the ten frame as shown. Write the numbers and trace the symbol to show the sets that are put together.

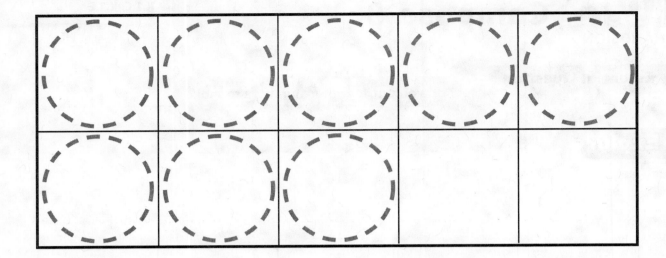

8   ___ ___ + ___ ___

2

8   ___ ___ + ___ ___

DIRECTIONS   **1.** Place counters in the ten frame to model numbers put together to make 8. How many are there of each color counter? Write the numbers and trace the symbol.   **2.** Place counters in the ten frame to model numbers put together to make 8. Write the numbers and trace the symbol. Draw and color the counters to match the numbers.

336 three hundred thirty-six

Name _____

3

8   _____   ╬   _____
        ----------   ----------
        _____   _____

4

8   _____   ╬   _____
        ----------   ----------
        _____   _____

DIRECTIONS   3. Place counters in the ten frame to model numbers put together to make 8. Write the numbers and trace the symbol.   **4.** Draw and color counters to model numbers put together to make 8. Write the numbers and trace the symbol.

HOME ACTIVITY • Show your child 8 objects. Have your child break apart the set to show the different ways to make eight.

Problem Solving Real World

5

$$8 \quad \underline{} + \underline{}$$

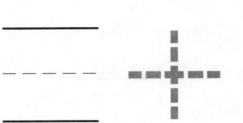

Daily Assessment Task

6

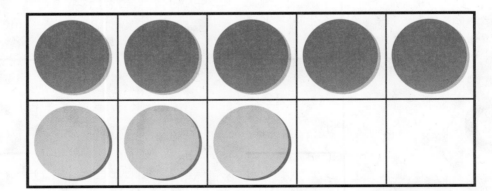

○ **5 + 3**   ○ **2 + 6**

DIRECTIONS **5.** Madison has 8 counters. 6 of her counters are yellow. The rest are red. How many are red? Draw to solve the problem. Write the numbers and trace the symbol. **6.** Count the counters. Which numbers are put together? Choose the right answer.

338 three hundred thirty-eight

TEKS **Number and Operations—K.2.I**
Also K.2.B, K.2.C, K.2.D
MATHEMATICAL PROCESSES K.1.C

Name _____

10.2
HANDS ON

Compose 8

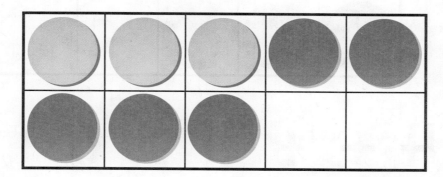

8

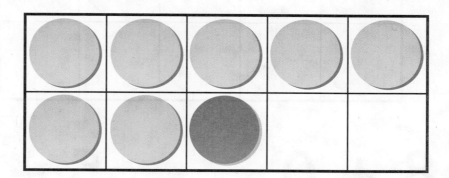

8

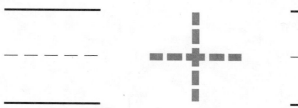

DIRECTIONS **1–2.** Count the counters in the ten frame that model numbers put together. How many are there of each color counter? Write the numbers and trace the symbol.

3

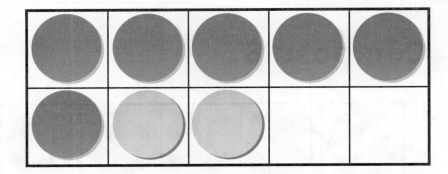

○ 4 + 4   ○ 6 + 2

4

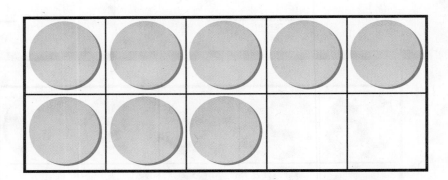

○ 8 + 0   ○ 5 + 3

DIRECTIONS Choose the correct answer.
3–4. Count the counters. Which numbers are put together?

Name _____

Compose 9

TEKS Number and Operations—K.2.I
Also K.2.B, K.2.C, K.2.D
MATHEMATICAL PROCESSES
K.1.C, K.1.E

? **Essential Question**

How do you put together number pairs to make 9?

Explore

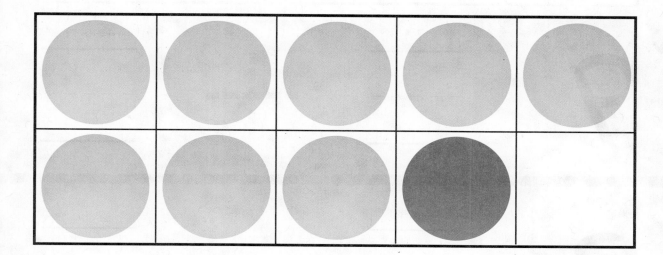

9   ____ + ____
     ____   ____

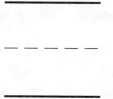

DIRECTIONS Place yellow and red counters in the ten frame as shown. Write the numbers and trace the symbol to show the number pair for 9.

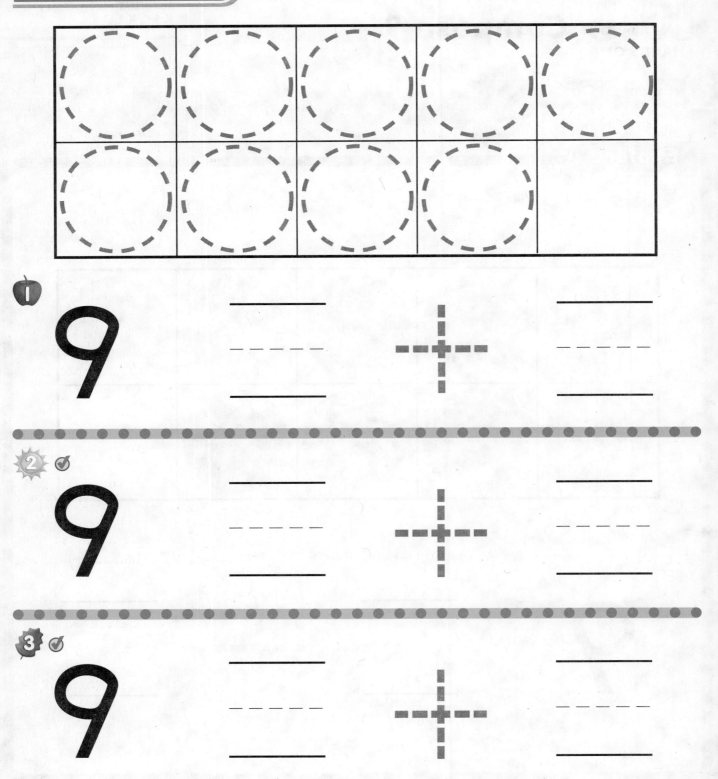

1 9 _____ + _____

2 ✓ 9 _____ + _____

3 ✓ 9 _____ + _____

DIRECTIONS Use counters to show number pairs that make 9.
1–3. Write the number pair and trace the symbol. For Exercise 3, color the counters to model the number pair that makes 9.

Name _____

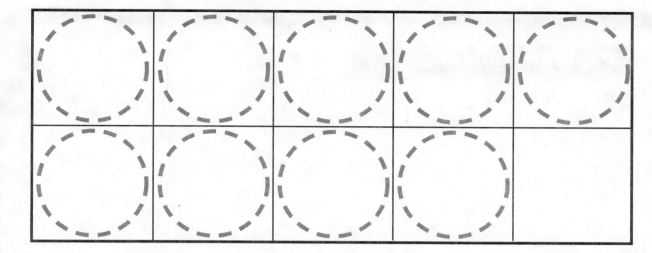

4

9   _____   **+**   _____

5

9   _____   **+**   _____

6

9   _____   **+**   _____

DIRECTIONS Use counters to show number pairs that make 9. **4–6.** Write the number pair and trace the symbol. For Exercise 6, color the counters to model the number pair that makes 9.

 HOME ACTIVITY • Have your child use his or her fingers on two hands to show a number pair for 9.

Module 10 • Lesson 3   three hundred forty-three **343**

Problem Solving Real World

7

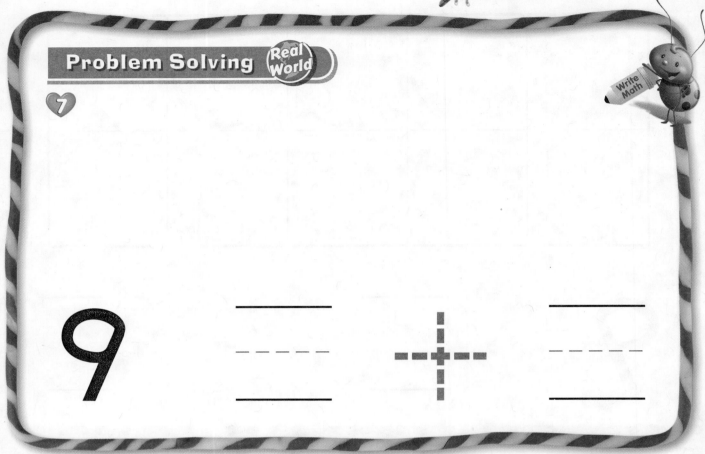

9 ＿＿＿ ＋ ＿＿＿

Daily Assessment Task

8

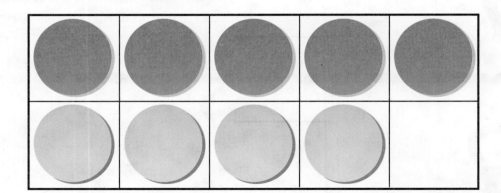

○ **5 + 4**   ○ **3 + 6**

DIRECTIONS **7.** Shelby has nine counters. None of them are red. The rest are yellow. How many are yellow? Draw to solve the problem. Write the numbers and trace the symbol. **8.** Choose the correct answer. Count the counters. Which number pair is shown?

TEKS **Number and Operations—K.2.I**
Also K.2.B, K.2.C, K.2.D
MATHEMATICAL PROCESSES **K.1.C**

Name _____

10.3 HANDS ON · Compose 9

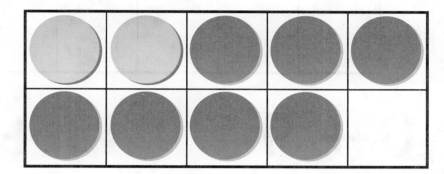

9   _ _ _ _ _ _ + _ _ _ _ _

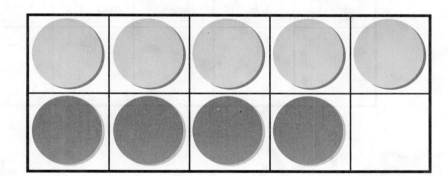

9   _ _ _ _ _ _ + _ _ _ _ _

DIRECTIONS 1–2. Count the counters in the ten frame that model the number pair that makes 9. Write the number pair and trace the symbol.

 3

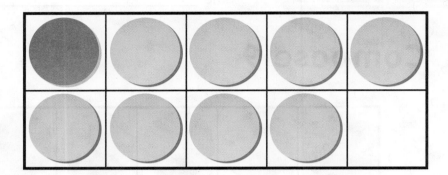

○ **0 + 9**　　　○ **1 + 8**

 4

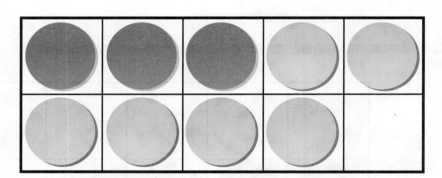

○ **3 + 6**　　　○ **2 + 7**

DIRECTIONS Choose the correct answer.
3–4. Count the counters. Which number pair is shown?

346 three hundred forty-six

TEKS Number and
Operations—K.2.I
Also K.2.B, K.2.C, K.2.D
MATHEMATICAL PROCESSES
K.1.C, K.1.E

10.4
HANDS ON

Compose 10

? **Essential Question**

How do you put together numbers to make 10?

Explore

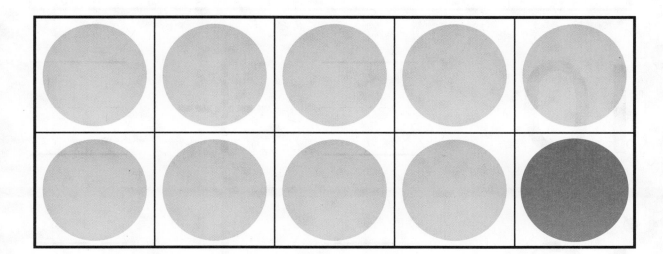

10

DIRECTIONS Place yellow and red counters in the ten frame as shown. Write the numbers and trace the symbol to show the number pair for 10.

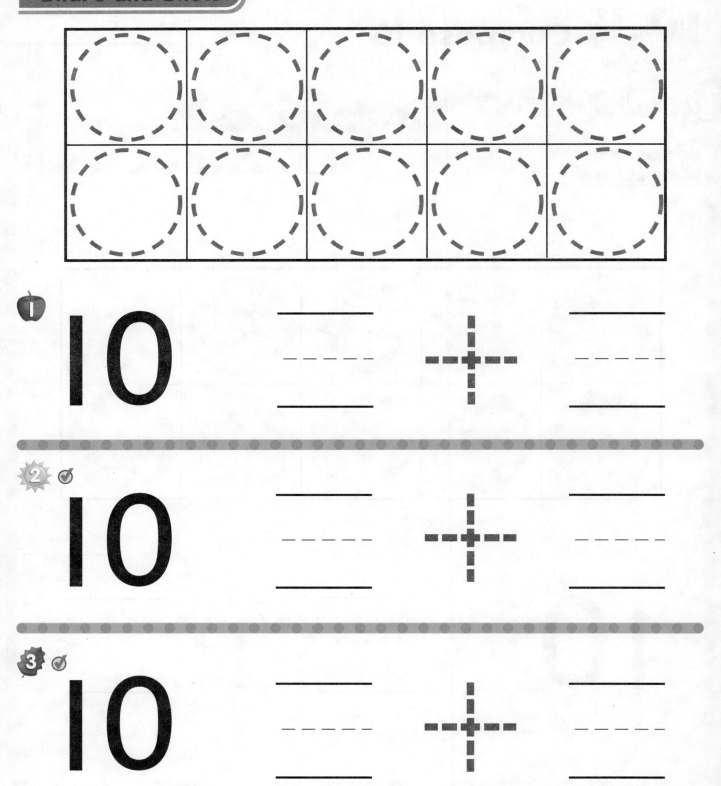

1 10 _____ + _____

2 ✓ 10 _____ + _____

3 ✓ 10 _____ + _____

DIRECTIONS Use counters to show number pairs that make 10.
1–3. Write the number pair and trace the symbol. For Exercise 3, color the counters to model the number pair that makes 10.

Name _____

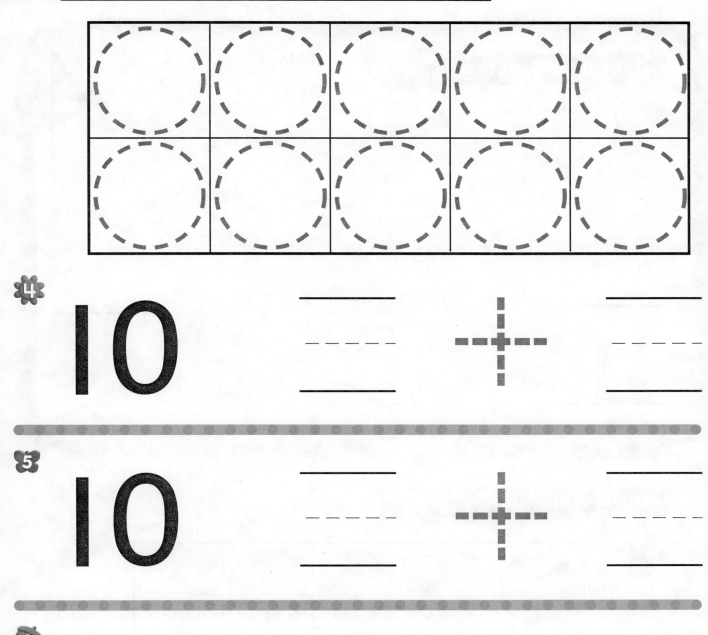

4 10 _____ + _____

5 10 _____ + _____

6 10 _____ + _____

DIRECTIONS Use counters to show number pairs that make 10. **4–6.** Write the number pair and trace the symbol. For Exercise 6, color the counters to model the number pair that makes 10.

HOME ACTIVITY • Have your child use his or her fingers on two hands to show a number pair for 10.

Problem Solving Real World

7

Daily Assessment Task

8

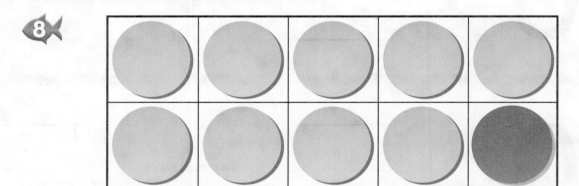

○ 9 + 1   ○ 5 + 5

DIRECTIONS 7. Riley has 9 red counters and 1 yellow counter. How many counters does she have? Draw to solve the problem. Write the numbers and trace the symbol. **8.** Choose the correct answer. Count the counters. Which number pair is shown?

TEKS Number and Operations—K.2.I
Also K.2.B, K.2.C, K.2.D
MATHEMATICAL PROCESSES K.1.C

Name _____

10.4
HANDS ON

Compose 10

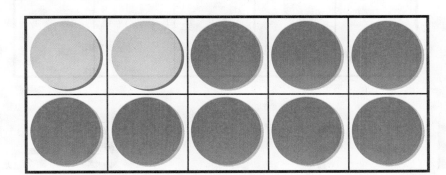

10   _____ + _____

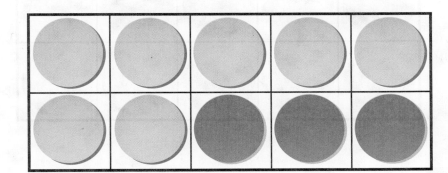

10   _____ + _____

DIRECTIONS 1–2. Count the counters in the ten frame that model the number pair that makes 10. Write the number pair and trace the symbol.

Module 10

three hundred fifty-one **351**

3

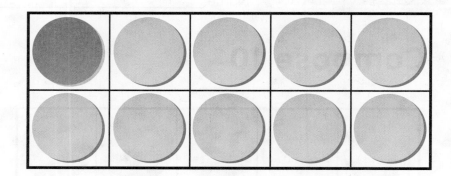

○ 1 + 9   ○ 6 + 4

4

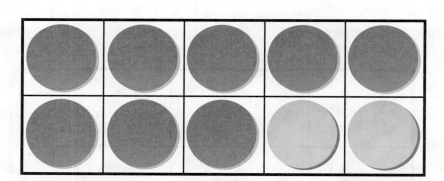

○ 5 + 5   ○ 8 + 2

DIRECTIONS Choose the correct answer.
3–4. Count the counters. Which number pair is shown?

TEKS Number and
Operations—K.2.I
Also K.2.B, K.2.C, K.2.D
MATHEMATICAL PROCESSES
K.1.C, K.1.D

10.5 HANDS ON Decompose 6 and 7

? Essential Question

How do you take away numbers from 6 and 7?

Explore

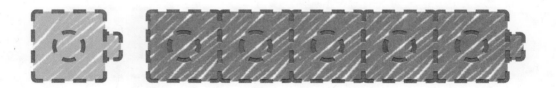

6 -- ___ ___

DIRECTIONS Model a six-cube train. One cube is yellow and the rest are red. Take apart the train to model the set taken apart. Draw and color the cube trains. Trace the symbol and write the numbers to show 6 taken apart.

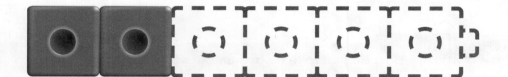

6 --

_____   _____

- - - - - -   - - - - - -

_____   _____

6 --

_____   _____

- - - - - -   - - - - - -

_____   _____

DIRECTIONS **I.** Model a six-cube train. Two cubes are blue and the rest are green. Take apart the train to model the set taken apart. Draw and color the cube trains. Trace the symbol and write the numbers to show 6 taken apart. **2.** Model a six-cube train. One cube is orange and the rest are blue. Take apart the train to model the set taken apart. Draw and color the cube trains. Trace the symbol and write the numbers to show 6 taken apart.

7 − _____ = _____   _____

7 − _____ = _____   _____

DIRECTIONS 3. Model a seven-cube train. Three cubes are red and the rest are blue. Take apart the train to model the set taken apart. Draw and color the cube trains. Trace the symbol and write the numbers to show 7 taken apart. **4.** Model a seven-cube train. Five cubes are yellow and the rest are green. Take apart the train to model the set taken apart. Draw and color the cube trains. Trace the symbol and write the numbers to show 7 taken apart.

HOME ACTIVITY • Show your child six or seven small objects. Take apart the set of objects. Have him or her tell a word problem to match the subtraction.

Problem Solving

5

7 − _____ = _____

Daily Assessment Task

6

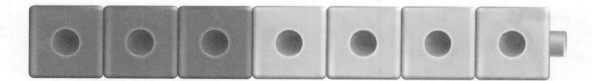

○ 4 − 3   ○ 7 − 3

DIRECTIONS **5.** Juli has seven erasers. One eraser is blue. The rest of the erasers are pink. How many erasers are pink? Draw the erasers. Trace the symbol and write the numbers. **6.** Choose the correct answer. Which does the cube train show?

356 three hundred fifty-six

TEKS Number and Operations—K.2.I
Also K.2.B, K.2.C, K.2.D
MATHEMATICAL PROCESSES **K.1.D**

Name _____

10.5 HANDS ON
Decompose 6 and 7

6 -- _____ _____

7 -- _____ _____

> **DIRECTIONS 1.** Look at the six-cube train. Three cubes are orange. The rest are green. Take apart the train by drawing to model the set taken apart. Color the cube trains. Trace and write to show 6 taken apart. **2.** Look at the seven-cube train. Two cubes are blue. The rest are yellow. Take apart the train by drawing to model the set taken apart. Color the cube trains. Trace and write to show 7 taken apart.

Lesson Check

TEXAS Test Prep

3

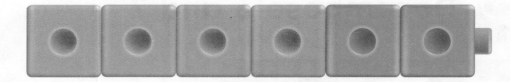

○ 4 – 2 ○ 6 – 4

4

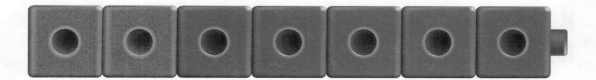

○ 7 – 2 ○ 5 – 2

DIRECTIONS 3–4. Choose the correct answer. Which does the cube train show?

Name _____

10.6
HANDS ON

Decompose 8 and 9

 Essential Question   How do you take away numbers from 8 and 9?

Explore

8 --- _____   _____

DIRECTIONS Model an eight-cube train. One cube is yellow and the rest are red. Take apart the train to model the set taken apart. Draw and color the cube trains. Trace the symbol and write the numbers to show 8 taken apart.

8 --- _____ _____

8 --- _____ _____

DIRECTIONS **1.** Model an eight-cube train. Two cubes are blue and the rest are green. Take apart the train to model the set taken apart. Draw and color the cube trains. Trace the symbol and write the numbers to show 8 taken apart. **2.** Model an eight-cube train. Three cubes are orange and the rest are blue. Take apart the train to model the set taken apart. Draw and color the cube trains. Trace the symbol and write the numbers to show 8 taken apart.

Name _____

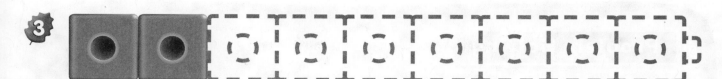

9 -- ____ ____
     ---- ----
     ____ ____

9 -- ____ ____
     ---- ----
     ____ ____

DIRECTIONS 3. Model a nine-cube train. Two cubes are red and the rest are blue. Take apart the train to model the set taken apart. Draw and color the cube trains. Trace the symbol and write the numbers to show 9 taken apart. **4.** Model a nine-cube train. Four cubes are orange and the rest are green. Take apart the train to model the set taken apart. Draw and color the cube trains. Trace the symbol and write the numbers to show 9 taken apart.

HOME ACTIVITY • Find 8 or 9 small household objects. Line them up and have your child take apart two sets. Have your child tell you how many objects are in each set.

Problem Solving

5

9 --- _____   _____

Daily Assessment Task

6

○ 9 – 6   ○ 6 – 3

....

DIRECTIONS **5.** Michelle has 9 cubes. 8 cubes are red. The rest of the cubes are blue. How many cubes are blue? Draw the cubes. Trace the symbol and write the numbers.
6. Choose the correct answer. Which does the cube train show?

TEKS Number and Operations—K.2.I
Also K.2.B, K.2.C, K.2.D
MATHEMATICAL PROCESSES **K.1.C**

Name _____

10.6
HANDS ON

Decompose 8 and 9

8 --- ‾ ‾ ‾ ‾   ‾ ‾ ‾ ‾

9 --- ‾ ‾ ‾ ‾   ‾ ‾ ‾ ‾

DIRECTIONS I. Look at the eight-cube train. Four cubes are blue and the rest are red. Take apart the train by drawing to model the set taken apart. Color the trains. Trace and write to show 8 taken apart. **2.** Look at the nine-cube train. Six cubes are orange and the rest are green. Take apart the train by drawing to model the set taken apart. Color the trains. Trace and write to show 9 taken apart.

Lesson Check

TEXAS Test Prep

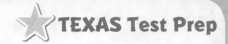

3

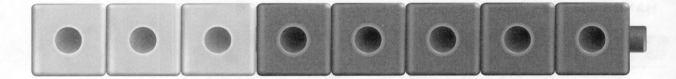

○ 5 – 3 ○ 8 – 3

4

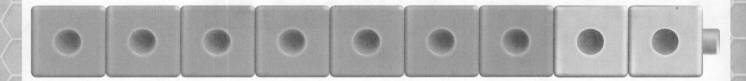

○ 9 – 7 ○ 7 – 2

DIRECTIONS **3–4.** Choose the correct answer. Which does the cube train show?

TEKS Number and Operations—K.2.I
Also K.2.B, K.2.C, K.2.D
MATHEMATICAL PROCESSES
K.1.D, K.1.E

10.7 HANDS ON Decompose 10

 Essential Question How do you take away numbers from 10?

Explore

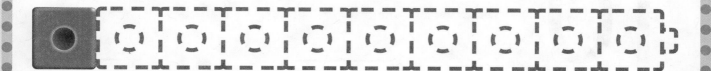

10 -- _____   _____

DIRECTIONS Model a ten-cube train. One cube is blue and the rest are red. Take apart the train to model the set taken apart. Draw and color the cube trains. Trace the symbol and write the numbers to show 10 taken apart.

10 --- _____ _____

2 ✓

10 --- _____ _____

DIRECTIONS 1. Model a ten-cube train. Three cubes are yellow and the rest are green. Take apart the train to model the set taken apart. Draw and color the cube trains. Trace the symbol and write the numbers to show 10 taken apart. **2.** Model a ten-cube train. Six cubes are orange and the rest are blue. Take apart the train to model the set taken apart. Draw and color the cube trains. Trace the symbol and write the numbers to show 10 taken apart.

366 three hundred sixty-six

10 -- _____ = _____

10 -- _____ = _____

DIRECTIONS 3. Model a ten-cube train. Two cubes are red and the rest are blue. Take apart the train to model the set taken apart. Draw and color the cube trains. Trace the symbol and write the numbers to show 10 taken apart. **4.** Model a ten-cube train. Five cubes are orange and the rest are green. Take apart the train to model the set taken apart. Draw and color the cube trains. Trace the symbol and write the numbers to show 10 taken apart.

HOME ACTIVITY • Ask your child to show a set of 10 objects, using objects of the same kind that are different in one way, for example, large and small paper clips. Then have him or her write the numbers that show how many of each kind are in the set.

Problem Solving

5

$$10 --- \underline{\hspace{3cm}} \quad \underline{\hspace{3cm}}$$

Daily Assessment Task

6

○ **5 – 5**   ○ **10 – 5**

DIRECTIONS **5.** Sydney has 10 square tiles. 8 of the tiles are red. The rest are yellow. How many tiles are yellow? Draw the tiles. Write the numbers and trace the symbol. **6.** Choose the correct answer. Which does the cube train show?

Name _____

10.7 HANDS ON Decompose 10

1

$$10 \quad \text{---} \quad \underline{} \quad \underline{}$$

2

$$10 \quad \text{---} \quad \underline{} \quad \underline{}$$

DIRECTIONS **1.** Look at the ten-cube train. Eight cubes are orange and the rest are yellow. Take apart the train by drawing to model the set taken apart. Color the cube trains. Trace and write to show 10 taken apart. **2.** Look at the ten-cube train. Seven cubes are blue and the rest are red. Take apart the train by drawing to model the set taken apart. Trace and write to show 10 taken apart.

Lesson Check

TEXAS Test Prep

3

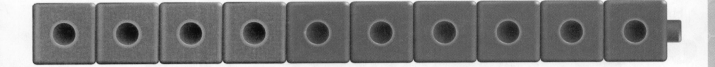

○ 10 – 4 ○ 6 – 4

4

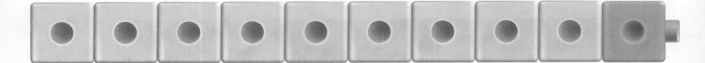

○ 9 – 1 ○ 10 – 9

DIRECTIONS Choose the correct answer.
3–4. Which does the cube train show?

Name _____

TEKS Number and Operations—K.2.I
Also K.2.B, K.2.C, K.2.D
MATHEMATICAL PROCESSES
K.1.E

10.8 PROBLEM SOLVING • Compose and Decompose Numbers up to 10

? **Essential Question** How can you solve problems using a picture?

Unlock the Problem

_____   _____   -+-   _____

DIRECTIONS There are some juice boxes for snack. Two of the juice boxes are orange juice. Six of the juice boxes are grape juice. How many juice boxes are there altogether? Use the picture to solve the problem. Write the numbers and trace the symbol.

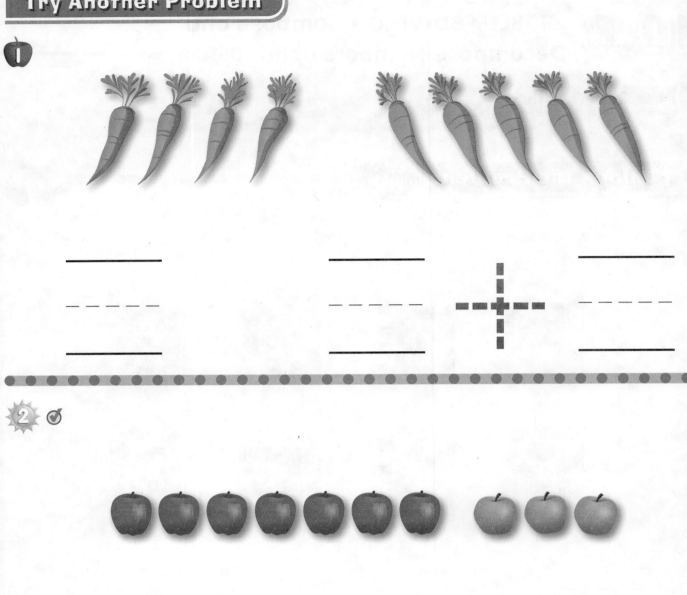

DIRECTIONS **1.** Monica has some carrots. She ate 4 carrots for snack. She ate 5 carrots for lunch. How many carrots did Monica eat? Use the picture to solve the problem. Write the numbers and trace the symbol. **2.** Some children brought in apples for snack. Seven apples are red. Three apples are green. How many apples are there? Use the picture to solve the problem. Write the numbers and trace the symbol.

Share and Show

3

_____   _____   _____

- - - -   ▬ ▬ ▬   - - - -   - - - -

_____   _____   _____

4

_____   _____   _____

- - - -   ▬ ▬ ▬   - - - -   - - - -

_____   _____   _____

DIRECTIONS **3.** There are six bananas on the snack table. Two bananas are green. How many bananas are yellow? Use the picture to solve the problem. Write the numbers and trace the symbol. **4.** Seven muffins are on the snack table. One is a blueberry muffin and the rest are cherry muffins. How many are cherry muffins? Use the picture to solve the problem. Write the numbers and trace the symbol.

HOME ACTIVITY • Have your child draw a set of ten or fewer balloons. Have him or her circle and mark an X on some balloons to show that they have popped. Then have your child tell a word problem to match.

Daily Assessment Task

5

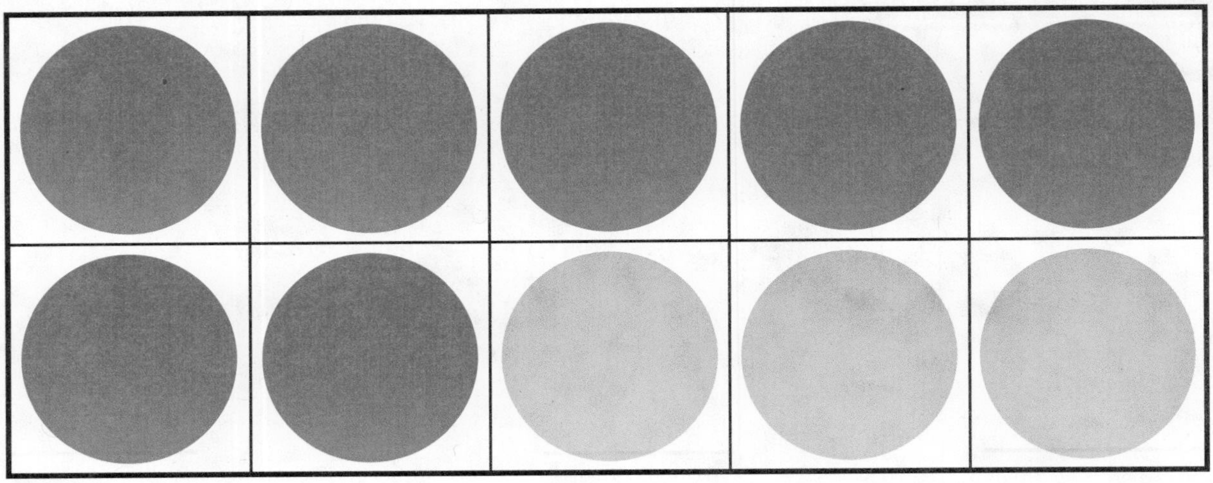

○ 7   ○ 10

6

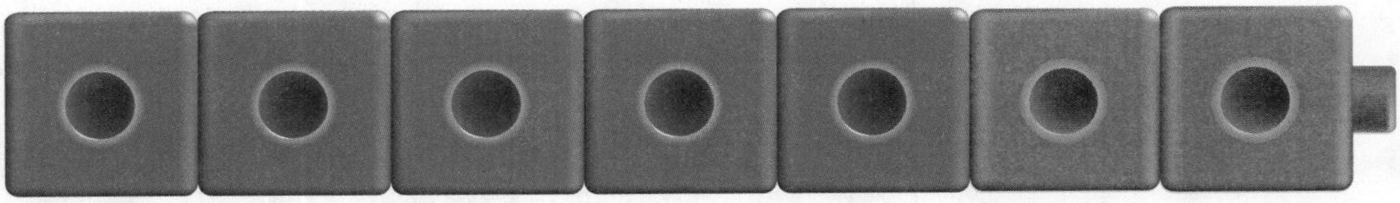

○ 5 – 2   ○ 7 – 5

7

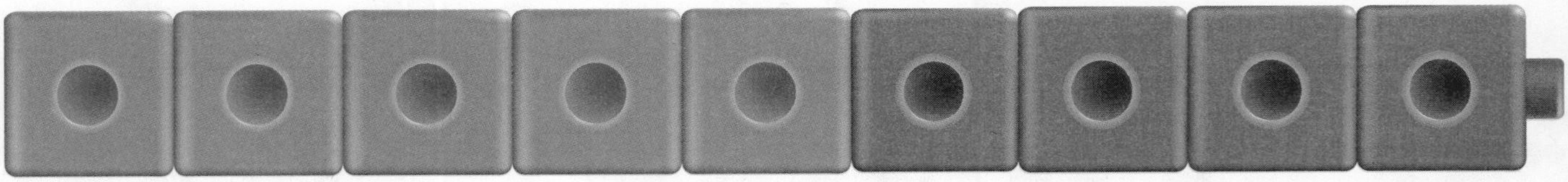

○ 4 + 4   ○ 5 + 4

DIRECTIONS **5.** There are 10 counters. How many counters will be left if you take apart 3? **6–7.** Which does the model show?

Name _____

10.8 PROBLEM SOLVING • Compose and Decompose Numbers up to 10

 **1**

_____   _ _ _ _ _   ✚   _ _ _ _ _

2

BLACK BLUE BROWN GREEN ORANGE PURPLE RED BLACK BLUE BROWN

_____   _ _ _ _ _   ▬ ▬   _ _ _ _ _   _ _ _ _ _

DIRECTIONS **1.** Carolyn had some pencils. She gave 3 pencils to her brother. She gave 6 pencils to her sister. How many pencils did Carolyn have? Use the picture to solve the problem. Write the numbers and trace the symbol. **2.** There are 10 crayons in the classroom. Six crayons are used for art class. How many crayons are left? Use the picture to solve the problem. Write the numbers and trace the symbol.

3

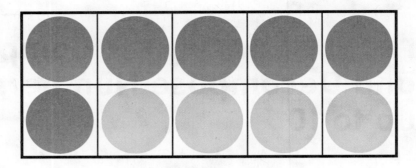

○ **5**   ○ **6**

4

○ **9 – 5**   ○ **5 – 4**

5

○ **2 + 5**   ○ **2 + 6**

DIRECTIONS Choose the correct answer.
3. There are 10 counters. How many counters will be left if you take away 4? **4–5.** Which does the model show?

Module 10 Assessment

Concepts and Skills

1

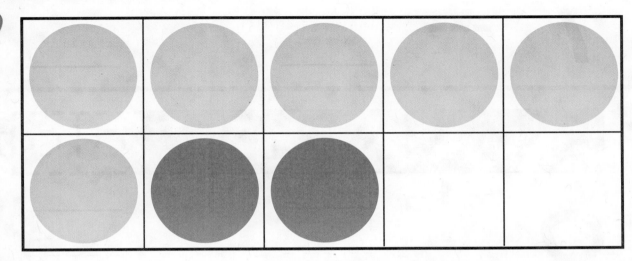

8

_ _ _ _ _ _   ╋   _ _ _ _ _ _

2

10

_ _ _ _ _ _   ╋   _ _ _ _ _ _

DIRECTIONS **1.** Count the counters in the ten frame. Write the number pair that makes 8. **2.** Look at the picture. Write the number pair that makes 10. ◆ TEKS K.2.I

3

7

4

9

---

5 ⭐ **TEXAS Test Prep**

___

- - - ▬▬▬

___

© Houghton Mifflin Harcourt Publishing Company

DIRECTIONS **3–4.** Use red and blue cubes to model the cube trains. Take apart the cube trains to model the set taken apart. Draw and color the cube trains. Trace the symbol and write the numbers. **5.** Kylee has some toy trucks. Four of the trucks are yellow. How many trucks are red? Write the numbers and trace the symbol. 🌟 TEKS K.2.I

378 three hundred seventy-eight

Name _____

11.1
HANDS ON ALGEBRA

Addition as Joining

? **Essential Question**

How can you show addition as joining?

Explore *Real World*

2 + 1 = ___

DIRECTIONS Listen to the addition word problem. Use counters. Trace the number that shows how many children are on the swings. Trace the *plus* symbol. Trace the number that shows how many children are being added to the group. Trace the *is equal to* symbol. Write the number that shows how many children there are now.

_____ + _____ === _____

DIRECTIONS **1.** Listen to the addition word problem. Use counters. Write the number that shows how many children are sitting, eating lunch. Trace the *plus* symbol and write the number that shows how many children are being added to the group. Trace the *is equal to* symbol and write the number that shows how many children are having lunch now.

Name _____

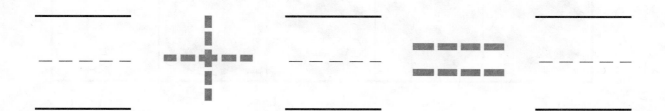

....

DIRECTIONS **2.** Listen to the addition word problem. Use counters. Write the number that shows how many children are playing with the ball. Trace the *plus* symbol and write the number that shows how many children are being added to the group. Trace the *is equal to* symbol and write the number that shows how many children there are now.

HOME ACTIVITY • Show your child a set of four objects. Have him or her add one object to the set and tell how many there are now.

Module 11 • Lesson 1

three hundred eighty-one **381**

Problem Solving Real World

3

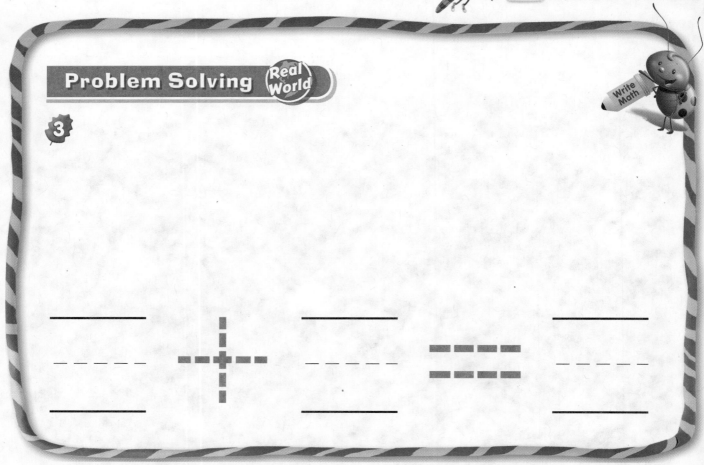

$$\underline{} + \underline{} = \underline{}$$

Daily Assessment Task

4

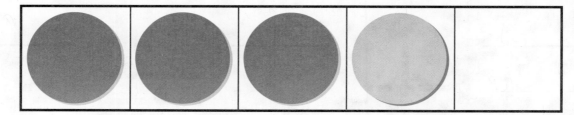

○ **3 + 1 = 4**   ○ **2 + 3 = 5**

DIRECTIONS 3. Two sheep are in a pen. Then two sheep are added to the pen. How many sheep are there now? Draw to show the sheep. Write the numbers and trace the symbols to complete the number sentence. **4.** Choose the correct answer. Which number sentence matches the model?

382 three hundred eighty-two

11.1 Addition as Joining

1

‒ ‒ ‒ ‒ ╋ ‒ ‒ ‒ ‒ ═══ ‒ ‒ ‒ ‒

DIRECTIONS I. Two children are playing with the sand. Two more children walk over to play. Write the number that shows how many children are playing. Write the number that shows how many children are being added to the group. Write the number that shows how many children there are now.

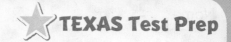

Lesson Check

★ TEXAS Test Prep

2

○ 2 + 2 = 4 ○ 2 + 3 = 5

3

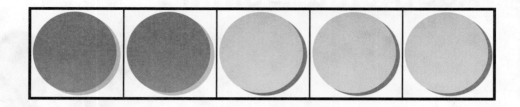

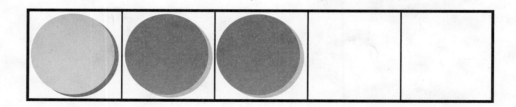

○ 1 + 2 = 3 ○ 1 + 1 = 2

DIRECTIONS Choose the correct answer.
2–3. Which number sentence matches the model?

TEKS Number and Operations—K.3.B

MATHEMATICAL PROCESSES
K.1.E

11.2 ALGEBRA More Addition

? **Essential Question** How can you solve addition word problems and complete the addition sentence?

Explore Real World

$$3 + 2 = \underline{\quad}$$

DIRECTIONS Listen to the addition word problem. Circle the set you start with. How many are being added to the set? How many are there now? Trace and write the addition sentence.

1

2

3 ✓

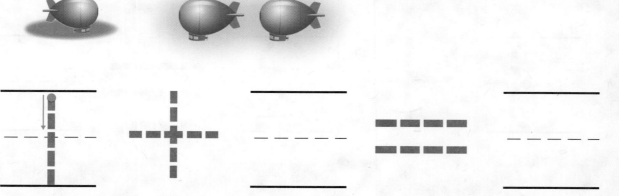

DIRECTIONS **1–3.** Listen to the addition word problem. Circle the set you start with. How many are being added to the set? How many are there now? Write and trace the numbers and symbols to complete the addition sentence.

Name _____

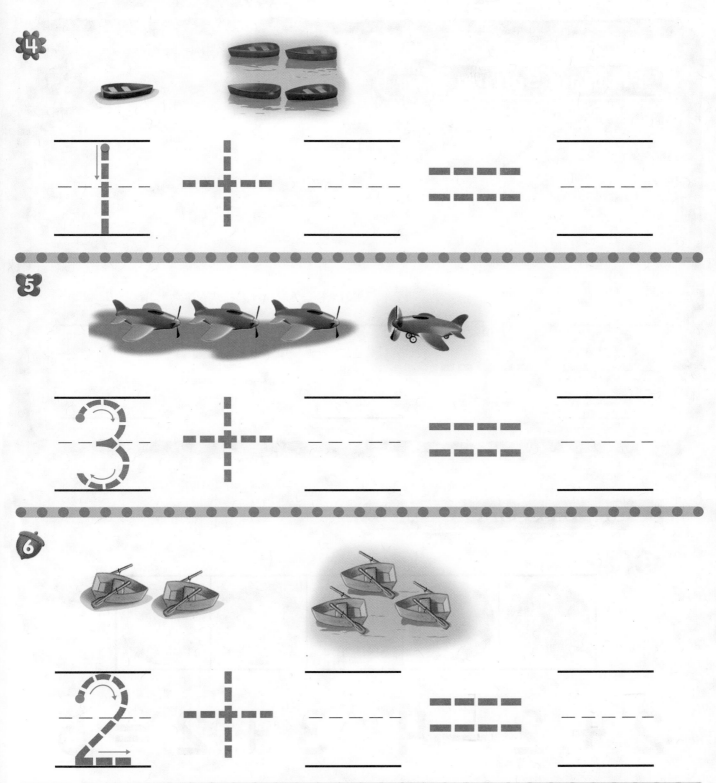

4

1 + ___ = ___

5

3 + ___ = ___

6

2 + ___ = ___

DIRECTIONS **4–6.** Tell an addition word problem about the sets. Circle the set you start with. How many are being added to the set? How many are there now? Write and trace the numbers and symbols to complete the addition sentence.

HOME ACTIVITY • Have your child show three fingers. Have him or her show more fingers to make five fingers in all. Then have your child tell how many more fingers he or she showed.

Module 11 • Lesson 2   three hundred eighty-seven **387**

Problem Solving Real World

$$2 + \text{\_\_\_} = \text{\_\_\_}$$

Daily Assessment Task

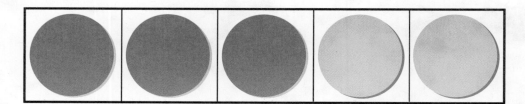

2 + 2 = 4   3 + 2 = 5
      ○   ○

DIRECTIONS 7. Bill catches two fish. Jake catches two more fish. How many fish do the
in all? Draw to show the fish. Trace and write to complete the addition sentence. **8.** Ch
correct answer. Which number sentence does the model show?

l show?

Name _____

DIRECTIONS   2. Listen to and use counters to act out the addition word problem. Write the numbers and trace the symbols to complete the addition sentence.

HOME ACTIVITY • Tell your child a short word problem about adding three objects to a set of two objects.. Have your child use toys to act out the word problem.

3

○ **2**

⊘ **1**

4

⊘ **4**

○ **3**

5

○ **2 + 1 = 3**   ⊘ **2 + 2 = 4**

DIRECTIONS Choose the correct answer. **3.** A fish is swimming. Another fish swims behind it. Act out 1 + 1. How many fish are there? **4.** Three birds are on a branch. Another bird joins them. Act out 3 + 1. How many birds are there? **5.** Two butterflies are on a flower. Two more butterflies come. Act out the problem. What does the picture show?

11.4 PROBLEM SOLVING • Addition Word Problems

TEKS **Number and Operations—K.3.C**
Also *K.3.B*
MATHEMATICAL PROCESSES **K.1.A**

1.

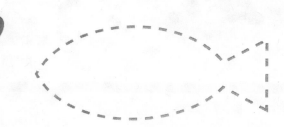

_____   **+**   _ _ _ _ _   **=**   _____

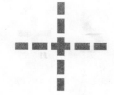 

DIRECTIONS **1.** One fish is swimming. Two more fish join. Draw to show the addition word problem. Write the numbers and trace the symbols to complete the addition sentence.

TEXAS Test Prep

○ **2**

⊘ **3**

⊘ **5**

○ **4**

◉ **3 + 1 = 4**   ○ **2 + 3 = 5**

DIRECTIONS Choose the correct answer.
2. Two puppies are eating. Another puppy joins
them. How many puppies are there? **3.** Three
ladybugs are on a leaf. Two more ladybugs join
them. How many ladybugs are there? **4.** Three
ducks are in a pond. One more duck comes. What
does the picture show?

Module 11 Assessment

Concepts and Skills

1

_____ + _____ === 3

2

3 + _____ === _____

3

1 + _____ === _____

DIRECTIONS **1.** Two cows are in a meadow. One more cow comes into the meadow. Write the numbers to show the cows being added. ⬇ TEKS K.3.A
2–3. Listen to the addition word problem. Circle the set you start with. How many are being added to the set? How many are there now? Trace and write the numbers and symbols to complete the addition sentence. ⬇ TEKS K.3.B

4

 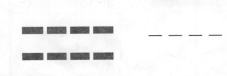

_____   **+**   - - - - -   **=**   - - - - -

- - - - -   _____   _____

  5

_____   **+**   - - - - -   **=**   - - - - -

- - - - -   _____   _____

6  ⭐ **TEXAS Test Prep**

○ **| + 2 = 3**

○ **2 + 3 = 5**

DIRECTIONS 4. There are four ducks swimming in a pond. One more duck comes. How many ducks are there? Write the number sentence. 🔶 TEKS K.3.B **5.** There are two squirrels by a tree. There are two more squirrels. How many squirrels are there altogether? Write the number sentence. **6.** Choose the correct answer. One bee is on a flower. Two more bees come. Act out the problem. What does the picture show? 🔶 TEKS K.3.C

TEKS Number and Operations—K.3.B
Also K.2.C, K.3.C

MATHEMATICAL PROCESSES
K.1.D, K.1.E

12.2
ALGEBRA

Write Subtraction

? **Essential Question**

How can you solve subtraction word problems and complete the subtraction sentence?

Explore *Real World*

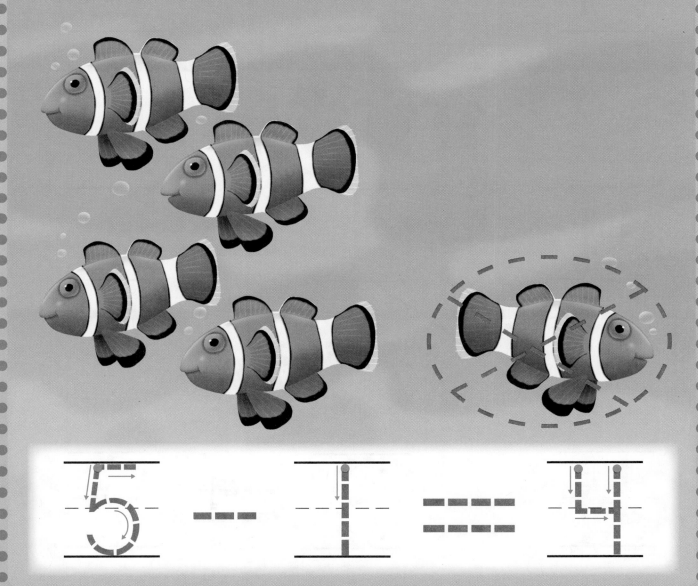

DIRECTIONS There are five fish. One fish swims away. How many fish are left? Trace the circle and X to show the fish swimming away. Trace the subtraction sentence.

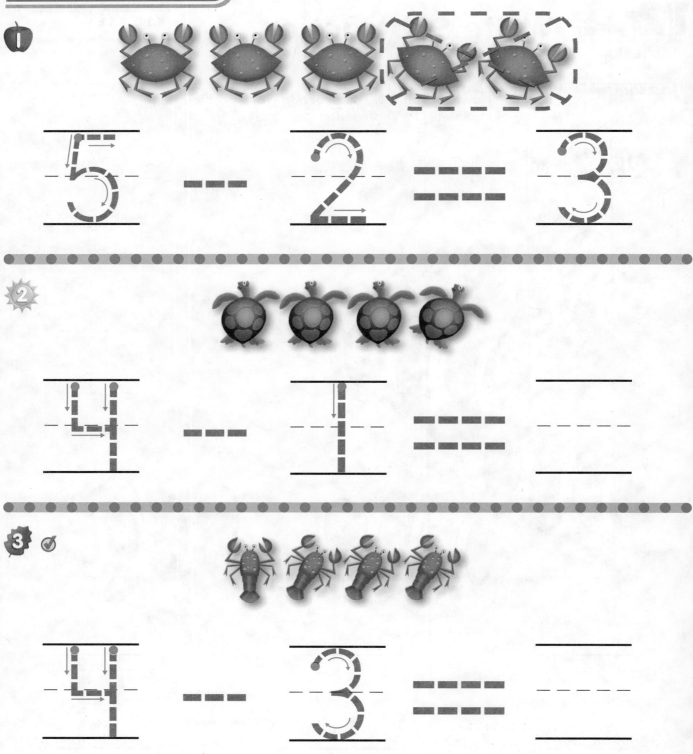

1

5 $-$ 2 $=$ 3

2

4 $-$ 1 $=$ ___

3

4 $-$ 3 $=$ ___

DIRECTIONS **1.** Listen to the subtraction word problem. Trace the circle and X to show how many crawl away. Trace to complete the subtraction sentence. **2–3.** Listen to the subtraction word problem. Draw a circle and mark an X to show how many leave. Trace and write to complete the subtraction sentence.

Name _____

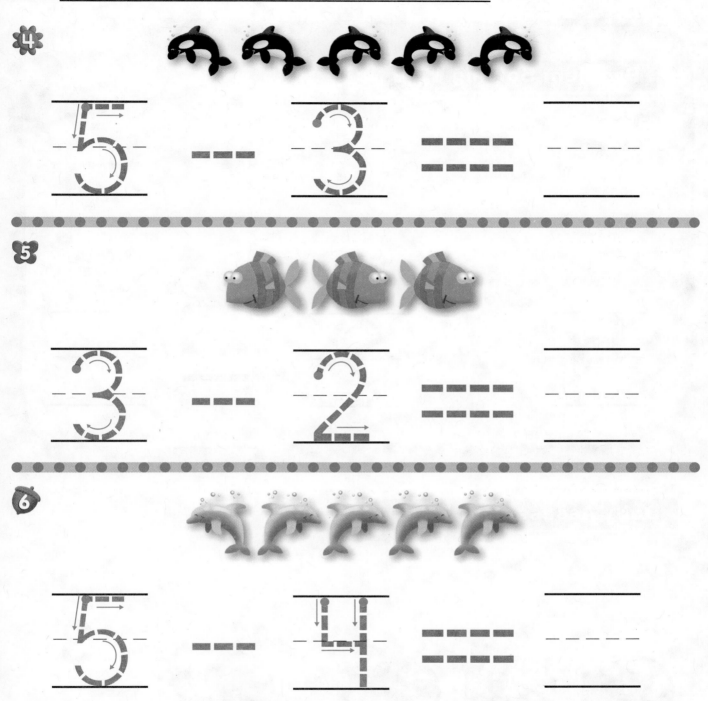

❋ 4

5 — 3 = _____

5

3 — 2 = _____

6

5 — 4 = _____

DIRECTIONS **4–6.** Listen to the subtraction word problem. Draw a circle and mark an X to show how many leave. Trace and write to complete the subtraction sentence.

HOME ACTIVITY • Have your child draw a set of five balloons. Have him or her circle and mark an X on some balloons to show that they have popped. Then have your child write a number sentence to show the subtraction.

Problem Solving

7

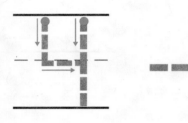   

Daily Assessment Task

8

○ **3**

○ **4**

DIRECTIONS **7.** Kristen has four flowers. She gives her friend two flowers. How many flowers does Kristen have now? Draw to solve the problem. Trace and write to complete the subtraction sentence. **8.** Choose the correct answer. There are four snails. One snail crawls away. What is 4 – 1?

Name _____

12.2
ALGEBRA

Write Subtraction

 1

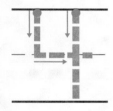 —  =

 2

 — 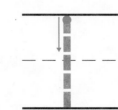 =

DIRECTIONS Listen to the subtraction word problem. Circle and mark an X to show how many leave. Trace and write to complete the subtraction sentence. **1.** There are four butterflies. Two fly away. How many are left? **2.** There are three kittens. One runs away. How many are left?

○ **5**

○ **4**

○ **2**

○ **3**

DIRECTIONS Choose the correct answer.
3. There are five bears. One bear leaves. What is
5 – 1? **4.** There are 4 kittens. Two kittens leave.
What is 4 – 2?

416 four hundred sixteen

TEKS Number and Operations—K.3.B
Also K.2.C, K.3.C
MATHEMATICAL PROCESSES
K.1.D, K.1.E

12.3
ALGEBRA

Differences Within 5

? **Essential Question**

How can you show differences within 5?

Explore Real World

DIRECTIONS There are four birds. One bird flies away. How many birds are left? Trace the circle and X to show the bird flying away from the set. Trace the subtraction sentence.

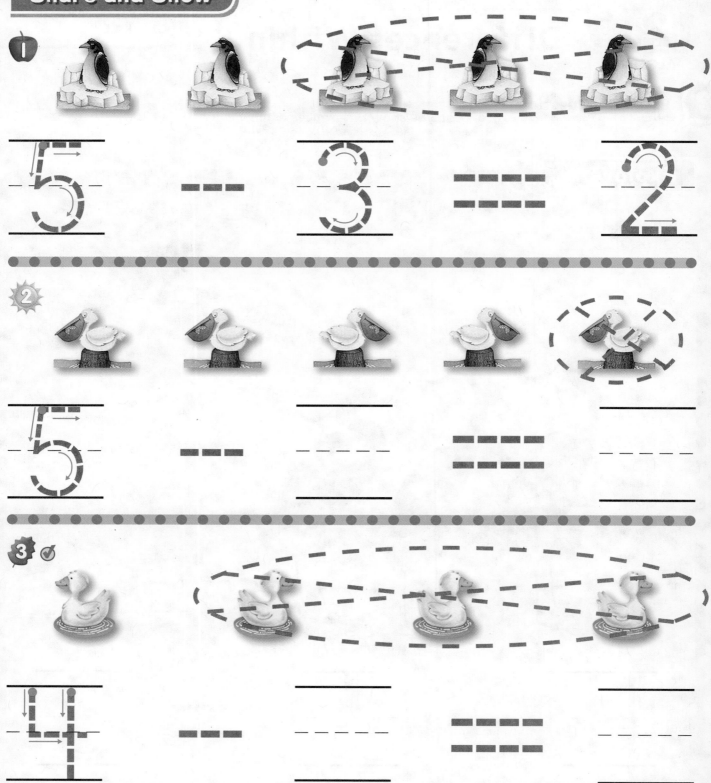

1 5 - 3 = 2

2 5 - ___ = ___

3 4 - ___ = ___

DIRECTIONS **1.** Listen to the subtraction word problem. How many penguins leave? Trace the circle and X. How many penguins are there now? Trace the subtraction sentence. **2–3.** Listen to the subtraction word problem. Trace the circle and X. Trace and write to complete the subtraction sentence.

Name _____

4

5 ___ ___ ___ ___

5

2 ___ ___ ___ ___

6

4 ___ ___ ___ ___

DIRECTIONS **4–6.** Listen to the subtraction word problem. Draw a circle and mark an X to show how many leave. Trace and write the numbers to complete the subtraction sentence.

 HOME ACTIVITY • Have your child tell a word problem for one of the subtraction sentences on this page.

Problem Solving

7

3 -- --- ═══ ┬

Daily Assessment Task

8

○ **3**

○ **1**

DIRECTIONS **7.** Draw to show what you know about this subtraction sentence. Tell a friend about your drawing. Complete the subtraction sentence. **8.** Choose the correct answer. There are five birds. Then two of the birds walk away. What is 5 – 2?

12.3 ALGEBRA Differences Within 5

5 -- ----- === -----

  ===

DIRECTIONS Listen to the subtraction word problem. Trace the circle and X. Trace and write the numbers to complete the subtraction sentence. **1.** There are five sheep. Two of the sheep run away. **2.** There are three squirrels. One squirrel runs away.

 **TEXAS Test Prep**

 Lesson Check

○ **3**   ○ **1**

○ **2**   ○ **3**

DIRECTIONS Choose the correct answer.
3. There are four trucks. Three trucks are driven
away. What is 4 – 3? **4.** There are 5 boats.
Three boats sail away. What is 5 – 3?

422 four hundred twenty-two

Name _____

TEKS Number and Operations—K.3.C
Also K.3.A, K.3.B
MATHEMATICAL PROCESSES
K.1.A, K.1.B

12.4
HANDS ON

PROBLEM SOLVING • Subtraction
Word Problems

? Essential Question

How can you solve problems using the strategy act it out?

DIRECTIONS Listen to and act out the subtraction word problem. Write the numbers and trace the symbols to complete the subtraction sentence.

_____   _____   _____

- - - - -   ▬▬▬   - - - -   ▬▬▬   - - - - -
                                   ▬▬▬

_____   _____   _____

DIRECTIONS **I.** Listen to and use cubes to act out the subtraction word problem. Write the numbers and trace the symbols to complete the subtraction sentence.

424 four hundred twenty-four

Name _____

2

- - - - - - - - - - - ▬▬▬ - - - - - - - - - - - - - ▬▬▬ - - - - - - -
                                                    ▬▬▬
_____   _____   _____

DIRECTIONS **2.** Listen to and use cubes to act out the subtraction word problem. Write and trace to complete the subtraction sentence.

HOME ACTIVITY • Tell your child a short subtraction word problem. Have him or her use objects to act out the word problem.

3

○ **2**

○ **1**

4

○ **3**

○ **5**

5

4 – 1 = 3   **5 – 2 = 3**
   ○   ○

DIRECTIONS Choose the correct answer. **3.** There are three children in a group. One child walks away. Use cubes to act out 3 – 1. How many children are left? **4.** There are five children. Then two children leave. Act out 5 – 2. How many children are left? **5.** There are four children. One child rolls away on skates. Act it out. What does the picture show?

12.4 PROBLEM SOLVING • Subtraction Word Problems

_____   _____   _____

- - - - -   ▬ ▬ ▬   - - - -   ▬ ▬ ▬   - - - - -
                                 ▬ ▬ ▬

_____   _____

DIRECTIONS I. There are 3 puppies in the basket. Juan takes one puppy out of the basket. How many puppies are left in the basket? Write the numbers and trace the symbols to complete the subtraction sentence.

2

○ **1**

○ **4**

3

○ **2**

○ **3**

4

○ **2**

○ **1**

DIRECTIONS Choose the correct answer.
2. There are five balloons. Four balloons fly away.
How many balloons are left? **3.** There are four
soccer balls. One soccer ball rolls away. How many
soccer balls are left? **4.** There are two frogs. One
frog hops away. How many frogs are left?

Name _____

Concepts and Skills

1

_____   _____   _____

- - - -   ▬ ▬ ▬   - - - -   ▬▬▬   - - - -

_____   _____   _____

2

_____   _____   _____

- - - -   ▬ ▬ ▬   - - - -   ▬▬▬   - - - -

_____   _____   _____

3

_____   _____   _____

4 ▬ ▬ 3 ▬▬▬ - - - -

_____   _____   _____

DIRECTIONS **1.** Four children are sitting together. Then one child leaves. Complete the subtraction sentence. ↳ TEKS K.3.A **2.** There are 5 children at a playground. Three children leave. How many children are there now? Write the subtraction sentence. ↳ TEKS K.3.A **3.** There are 4 seahorses. Three seahorses swim away. How many seahorses are left? Complete the subtraction sentence. ↳ TEKS K.3.B

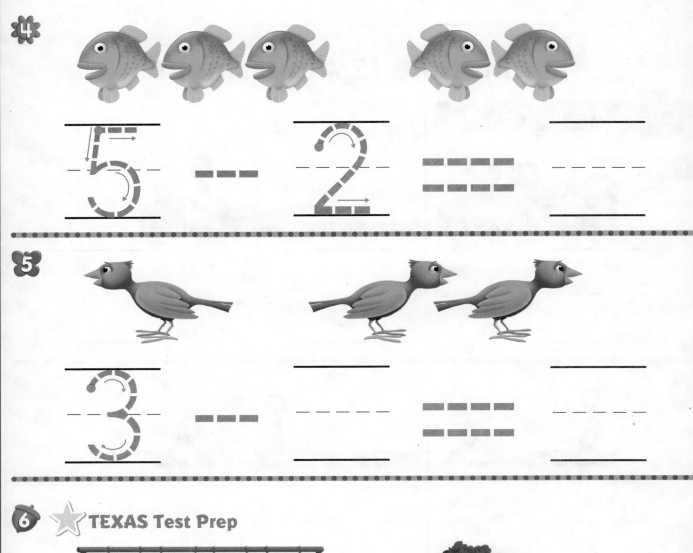

4

5 -- 2 === _

5

3 -- - === _

6

○ 5 − 3 = 2   ○ 4 − 2 = 2

DIRECTIONS **4.** There are 5 fish. Two fish swim away. How many fish are left? Circle and mark an X to show the fish that swim away. Complete the subtraction sentence. ↘ TEKS K.3.B **5.** There are 3 birds. Two birds fly away. How many birds are left? Circle and mark an X to show the birds that leave. Complete the subtraction sentence. ↘ TEKS K.3.B **6.** Choose the correct answer. There are 4 children on the swings. Then 2 children leave. Act out the problem. What does the picture show? ↘ TEKS K.3.C

TEKS Number and Operations—K.3.A, K.3.C Also K.2.F, K.3.B
MATHEMATICAL PROCESSES K.1.D

13.1
HANDS ON ALGEBRA

One More and One Less

? Essential Question How do you show one more and one less?

Explore

DIRECTIONS Place 5 blue cubes on the counter outline. Trace the number. Add 1 red counter. Write the number to show the sum. Place 5 blue cubes on the counter outline. Write the number. Take one counter away. Write the number to show the difference.

Share and Show

1

$6 + 1 =$ ____

2

$7 + 1 =$ ____

3

$8 + 1 =$ ____

4

$9 + 1 =$ ____

DIRECTIONS 1–4. Use two colors of cubes to show the sum. Write the number.

Name _____

5

10 − 1 = _____

6

9 − 1 = _____

7

8 − 1 = _____

8 ☑

7 − 1 = _____

DIRECTIONS **5–8.** Use two colors of cubes to show the difference. Write the number.

HOME ACTIVITY • Show your child a set of 5 to 10 toys. Have your child create a set of objects that shows one more and one less.

Problem Solving

9

_____ + | = _____

Daily Assessment Task

10

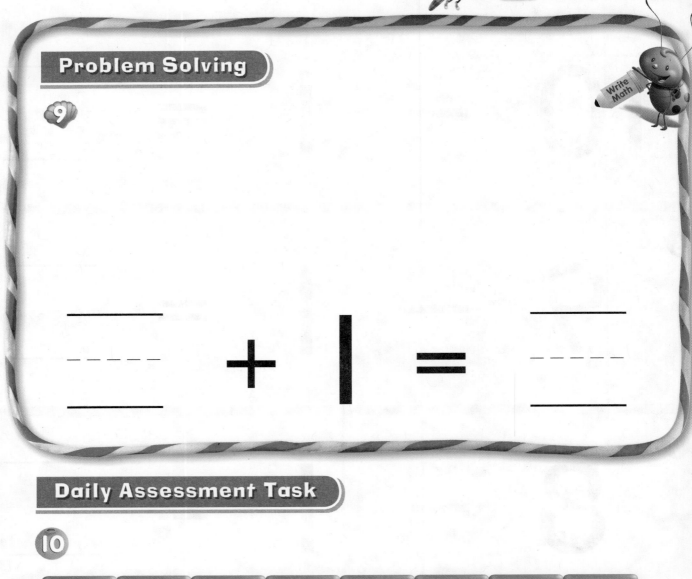

8 + | =

○ 7

○ 9

DIRECTIONS **9.** Wesley has 5 marbles. Draw to show how many marbles Wesley has. Write the number. Annie has I more marble than Wesley. How many marbles does Annie have? Write the number. **10.** Choose the correct answer. Lanie has 8 cubes. What number is one more?

434 four hundred thirty-four

13.1 I More and I Less

HANDS ON ALGEBRA

1

$$4 + 1 = \underline{\quad}$$

2

$$5 + 1 = \underline{\quad}$$

DIRECTIONS   1–2. Draw one more cube to show the sum. Use a different color. Write the sum.

Lesson Check

TEXAS Test Prep

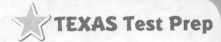

3

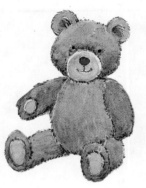

$3 + 1 =$

○ 4

○ 5

4

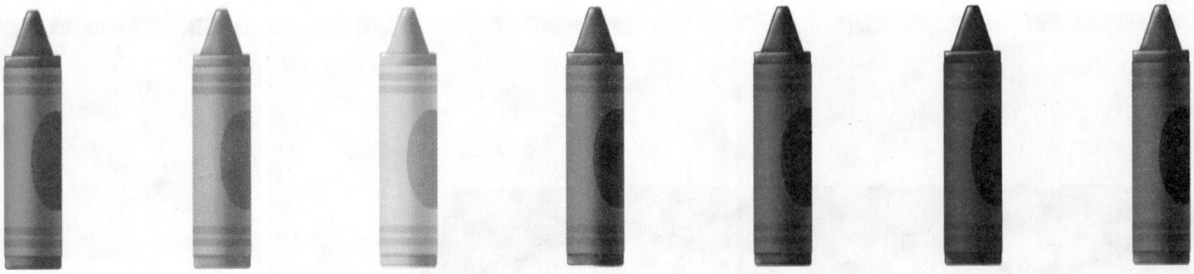

$7 - 1 =$

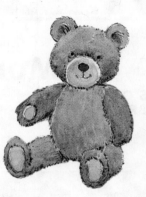

○ 8

○ 6

DIRECTIONS Choose the correct answer. **3.** Selena has 3 brown toy bears. What number is one more? **4.** Carlos has 7 crayons. What number is one less?

TEKS **Number and Operations—K.3.B**
Also K.3.C

MATHEMATICAL PROCESSES
K.1.D

13.3 Sums Up to 9
ALGEBRA

? Essential Question

How can you show and write addition sentences for sums to 9?

Explore

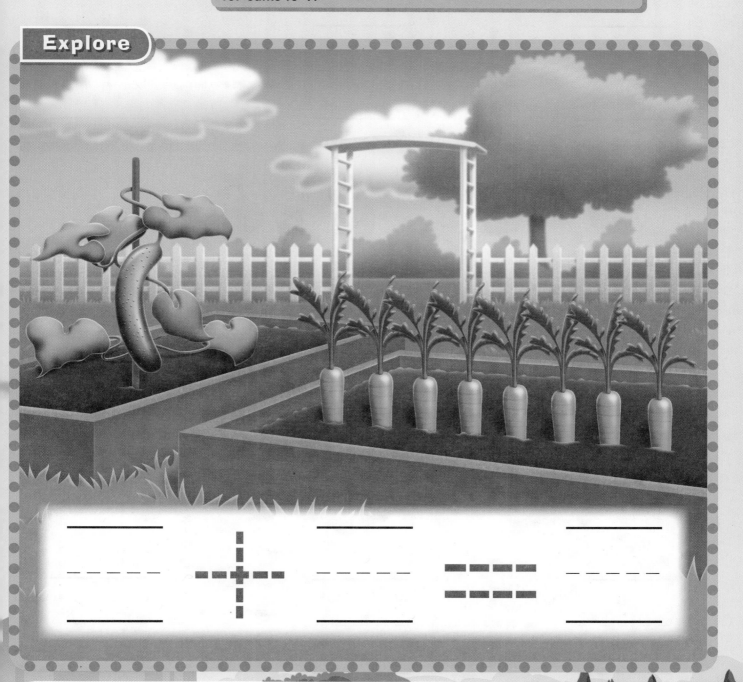

DIRECTIONS Listen to the addition word problem. Write the numbers to complete the addition sentence. Trace the symbols.

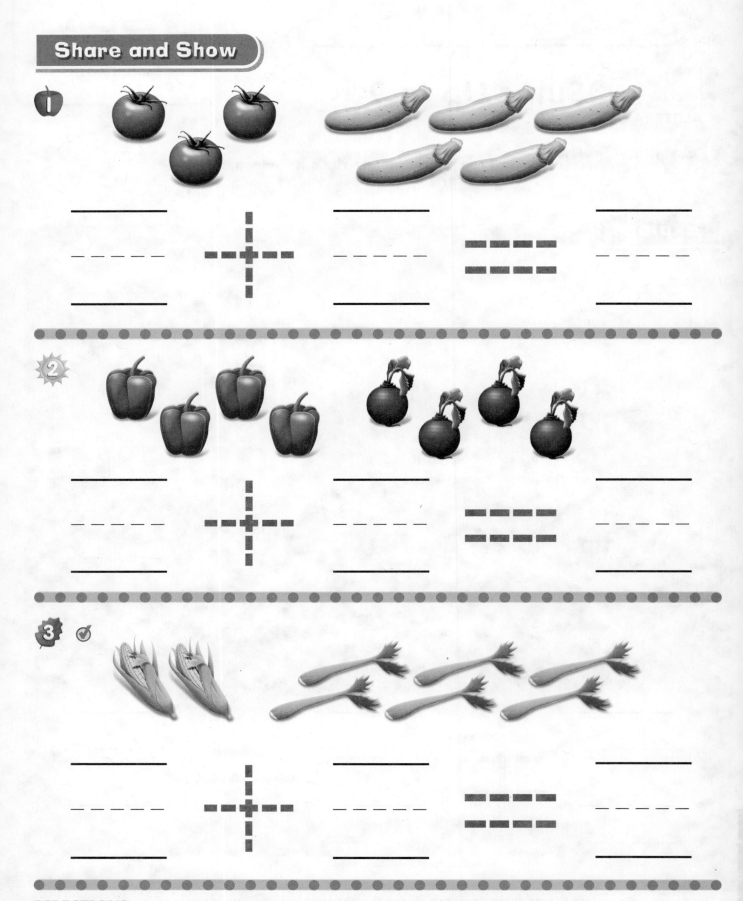

1

_____ + _ _ _ _ _____ = _ _ _ _

2

_____ + _ _ _ _ _____ = _ _ _ _

3

_____ + _ _ _ _ _____ = _ _ _ _

DIRECTIONS   1–3. Listen to the addition word problem. Complete the addition sentence.

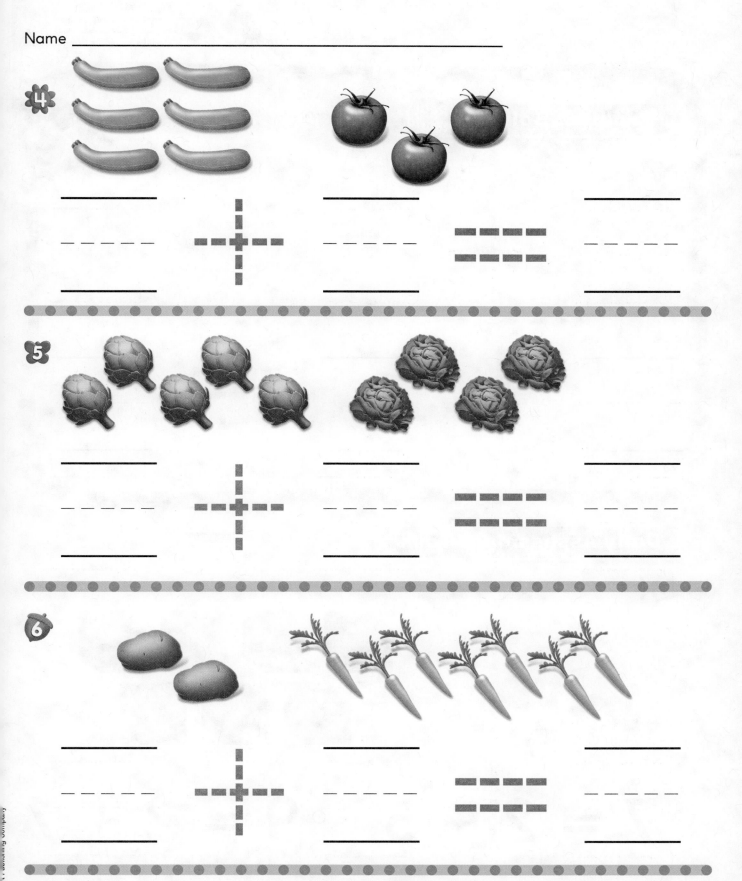

DIRECTIONS **4–6.** Listen to the addition word problem. Complete the addition sentence.

 HOME ACTIVITY • Have your child use his or her fingers on two hands to show two numbers and tell how many in all.

Module 13 • Lesson 3

four hundred forty-five **445**

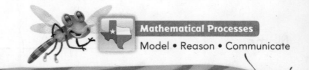

Problem Solving Real World

7

_____ **+** _ _ _ _ _ **═══** _ _ _ _ _

_____   _____   _____

Daily Assessment Task

 8

○ **7 = 2 + 5**   ○ **9 = 2 + 7**

• •

DIRECTIONS **7.** Shelby has nine counters. None of them are blue.
How many are red? Draw the counters. Complete the addition sentence.
8. Choose the correct answer. What does the picture show?

Name _____

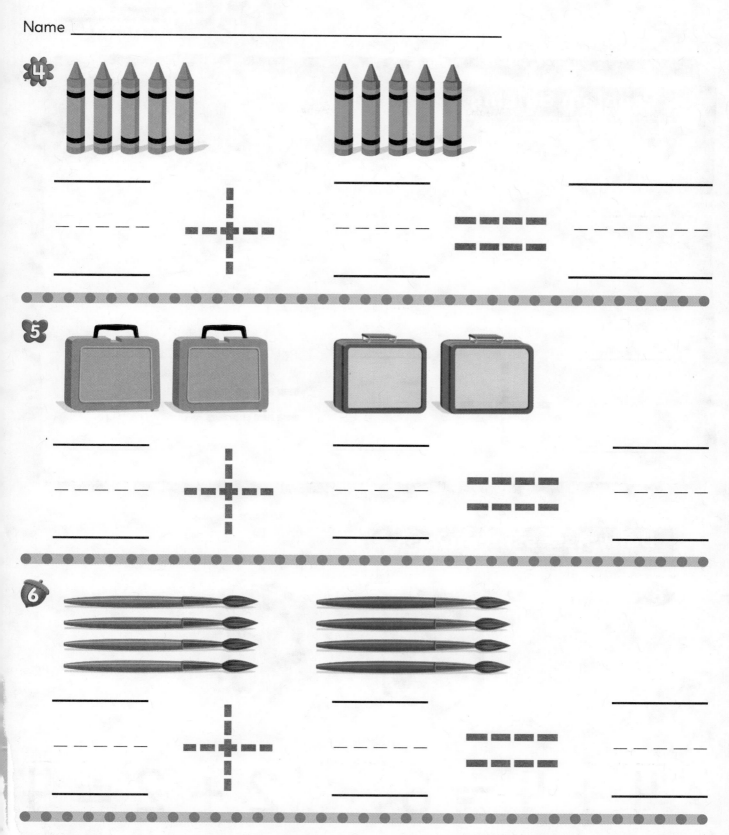

_____   +   _____ = _____

_____   +   _____ = _____

_____   +   _____ = _____

DIRECTIONS   **4–6.** Write the number in each group. Add. Write the sum. Trace the symbols.

HOME ACTIVITY • Show your child a set of 1 to 5 objects such as crayons. Have your child create a set of objects that shows the same number of objects and find the sum.

Module 13 • Lesson 5   four hundred fifty-seven   **457**

Problem Solving

7

Daily Assessment Task

 8

○ $4 + 4 = 8$　　○ $2 + 2 = 4$

DIRECTIONS **7.** Simon brought two snacks to school. Draw the snacks. Write the number. Clare brought two snacks to school. Draw the snacks. Write the number. How many snacks do they have together? Write the number. Trace the symbols. **8.** Choose the correct answer. What doubles addition does the picture show?

458 four hundred fifty-eight

Share and Show

❀ 4

_____   ╋   _____   ═   _____
- - - - - - - -   - - - - - - - -   - - - - - - - -
_____   _____   _____

✿ 5

_____   ╋   _____   ═   _____
- - - - - - - -   - - - - - - - -   - - - - - - - -
_____   _____   _____

❀ 6

_____   ╋   _____   ═   _____
- - - - - - - -   - - - - - - - - -   - - - - - - - -
_____   _____   _____

DIRECTIONS **4–6.** Listen to the addition word problem. Draw to show how many are in the set to start with. Write the number. Draw to show how many are being added. Write the number. Write the number in all.

○ **7**

○ **8**

○ **9**

○ **10**

○ **7 + 2 = 9**

○ **7 + 3 = 10**

DIRECTIONS Choose the correct answer. **7.** There are five caterpillars.
Two more join them. How many caterpillars are there now? **8.** Tom puts
5 toy bugs in the box. There were 4 bugs already in the box. How many bugs
are there now? **9.** Seven ladybugs are in a group. More ladybugs join them.
What number sentence does the picture show?

Name _____

13.6 PROBLEM SOLVING • Addition Word Problems

1

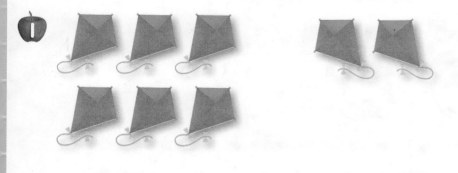

_____   +   - - - - -   =   - - - - -

2

_____   +   - - - - -   =   - - - - -

 3

○ **6**

○ **4**

4

○ **8**

○ **5**

5

○ **5 + 2 = 7**

○ **3 + 4 = 7**

DIRECTIONS Choose the correct answer.
3. Bill's mom buys 4 red apples. Then she buys 2 more. How many apples does she buy? **4.** Alan picks 2 ears of corn. Then he picks 3 more ears of corn. How many ears of corn does Alan pick?
5. Some frogs are sitting on a log. Then more frogs join them. What number sentence does the picture show?

Name _____

 Module 13 Assessment

Concepts and Skills

5 + 3 = _____

6 + 1 = _____

③

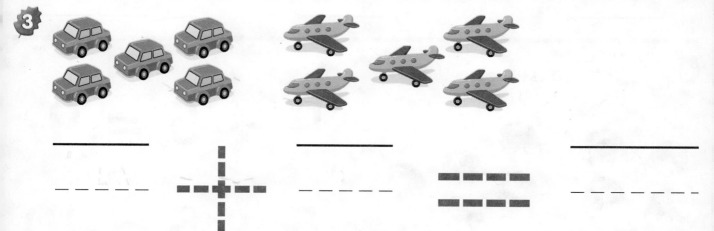

_____ + _____ = _____

DIRECTIONS 1–2. Complete the addition sentence. ✦ TEKS K.1.E, K.3.B
3. Keisha has five toy cars and five toy airplanes. How many toys does she have in all? ✦ TEKS K.1.A, K.3.B

Module 13   four hundred sixty-seven **467**

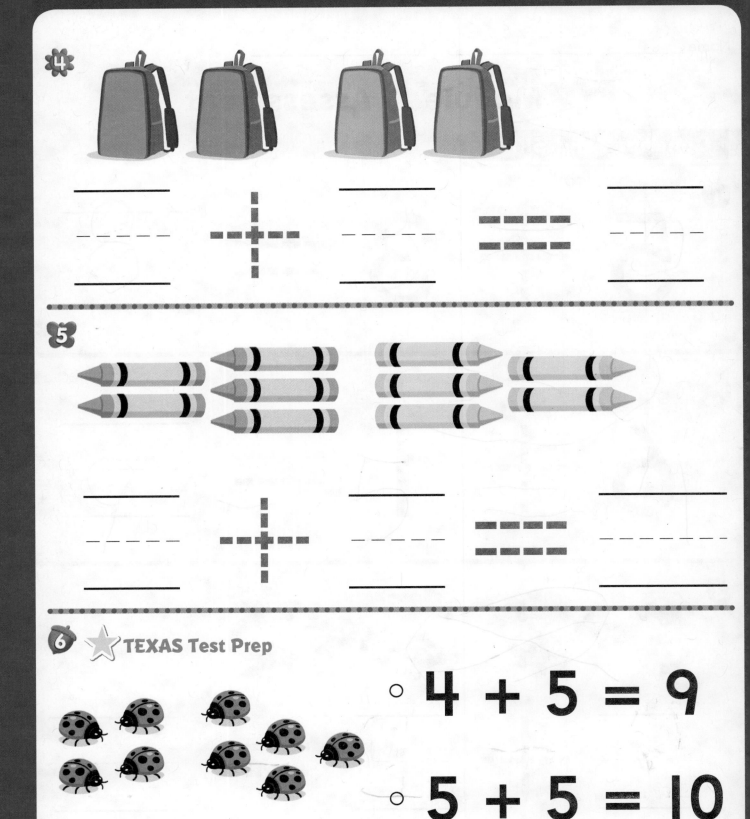

4

_____ + _____ = _____

5

_____ + _____ = _____

6 ⭐ **TEXAS Test Prep**

○ 4 + 5 = 9

○ 5 + 5 = 10

DIRECTIONS **4–5.** Write the number in each group. Add. Write the sum.
🔹TEKS K.1.D, K.3.C **6.** Choose the correct answer. There are four ladybugs.
Five more ladybugs came to join. How many ladybugs are there now? Which
addition sentence shows the story? 🔹TEKS K.1.B, K.3.C

Name _____

14.2 Differences Within 9

TEKS Number and Operations—K.3.B

MATHEMATICAL PROCESSES K.1.E

? Essential Question How can you show differences within 9?

$9 - 2 = 7$

DIRECTIONS There are nine cars. Two cars drive away. Trace the circle and X around those cars. How many cars are left? Trace and write to complete the subtraction sentence.

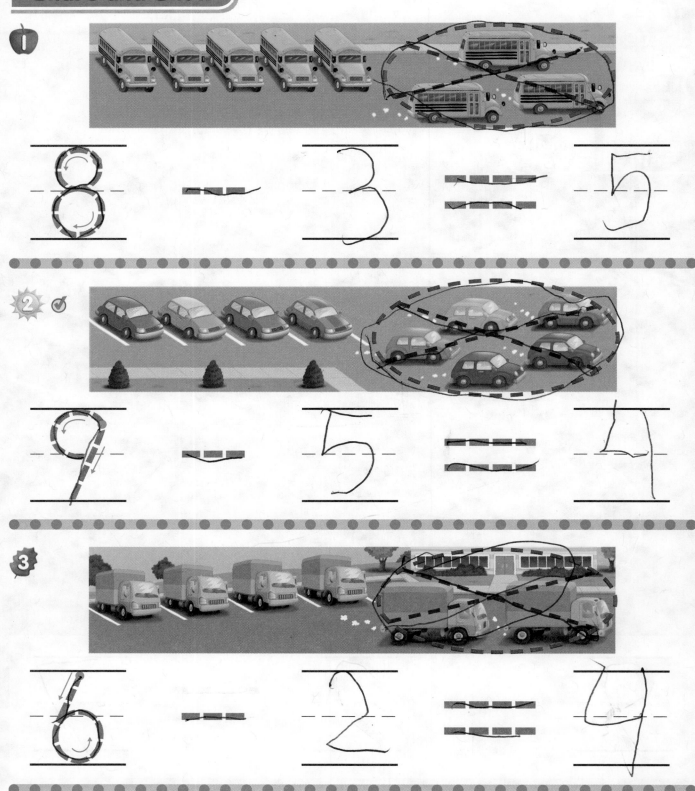

1. 8 − 3 = 5

2. 9 − 5 = 4

3. 6 − 2 = 4

DIRECTIONS 1. Listen to the subtraction word problem. How many buses drive away? Trace the circle and X. How many buses are left? Trace and write to complete the subtraction sentence. **2–3.** Listen to the subtraction word problem. Trace and write to complete the subtraction sentence.

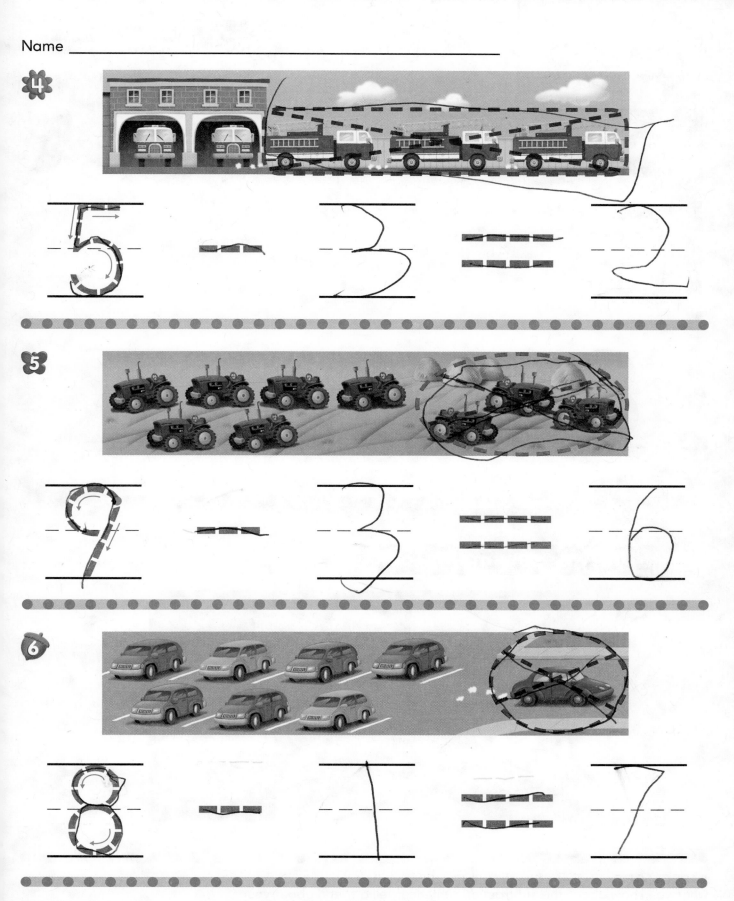

4.

5 − 3 = 2

5.

9 − 3 = 6

6.

8 − 1 = 7

DIRECTIONS **4–6.** Listen to the subtraction word problem.
Trace and write to complete the subtraction sentence.

Problem Solving

7

$$8 - 6 = \underline{\quad\quad}$$

Daily Assessment Task

○ 7

● 8

DIRECTIONS 7. Complete the subtraction sentence. Draw to show what you know about this subtraction sentence. Tell a friend about your drawing. **8.** Choose the correct answer. There are nine mail trucks. One mail truck drives away. What is 9 − 1?

478 four hundred seventy-eight

14.2 Differences Within 9

1

_9_ ___ − ___ ___ = = = ___ ___

2

_8_ ___ − ___ ___ = = = ___ ___

DIRECTIONS Trace and write to complete the subtraction sentence. **I.** There are nine motorcycles. Four motorcycles drive away. Trace the circle and X. How many motorcycles are left? **2.** There are eight bicycles. Four bicycles ride away. How many bicycles are left?

3

○ **8**

○ **6**

4

○ **3**

○ **9**

5

○ **5**

○ **4**

DIRECTIONS Choose the correct answer.
3. There are seven dump trucks. One dump truck drives away. What is 7 – 1? **4.** There are nine airplanes. Six airplanes fly away. What is 9 – 6?
5. There are eight sailboats. Four boats sail away. What is 8 – 4?

TEKS Number and Operations—K.3.B

MATHEMATICAL PROCESSES K.1.E

14.3 Differences Within 10

? Essential Question How can you show differences within 10?

Explore

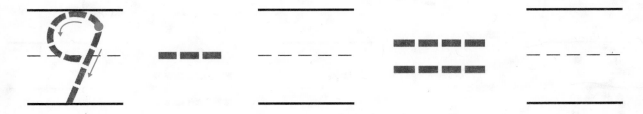

DIRECTIONS There are nine flowers. Four flowers are purple. Trace the circle and X around those flowers. The rest of the flowers are yellow. How many flowers are yellow? Trace and write to complete the subtraction sentence.

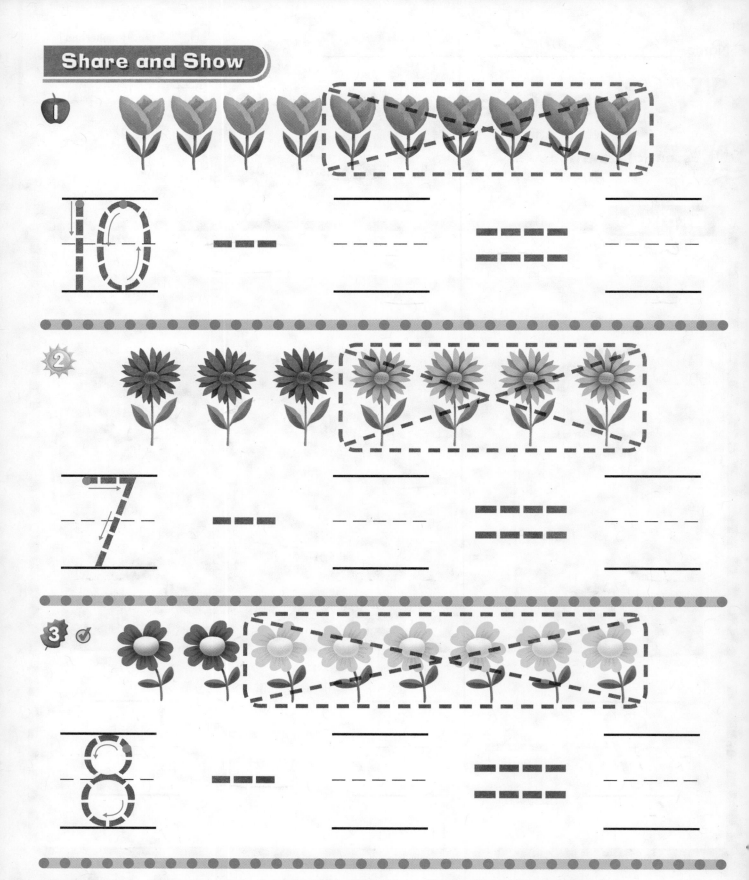

DIRECTIONS **I.** Listen to the subtraction word problem. There are ten flowers. Six of the flowers are orange. The rest are pink. Trace the circle and X. How many flowers are pink? Trace and write to complete the subtraction sentence. **2–3.** Listen to the subtraction word problem. Trace and write to complete the subtraction sentence.

Name ______________________

4

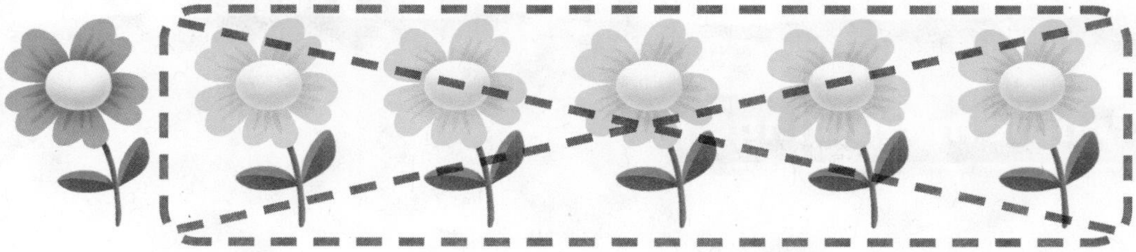

6 − ____ = ____

5

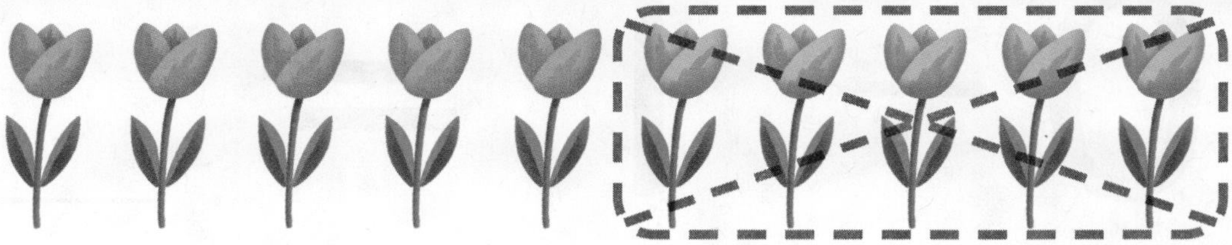

10 − ____ = ____

6

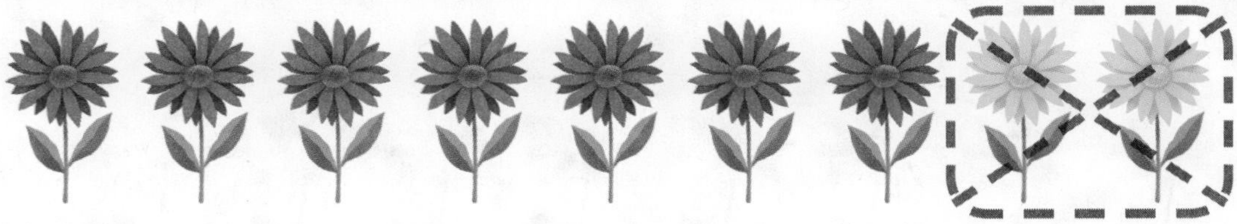

9 − ____ = ____

DIRECTIONS **4–6.** Listen to the subtraction word problem. Trace and write to complete the subtraction sentence.

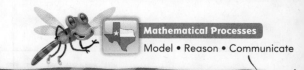
Problem Solving

♡ 7

10 − 1 = _____

Daily Assessment Task

🐟 8

○ **2**

○ **3**

DIRECTIONS 7. Complete the subtraction sentence. Draw to show what you know about this subtraction sentence. Tell a friend about your drawing. **8.** Choose the correct answer. There are nine flowers. Seven flowers are pink. The rest are yellow. What is 9 − 7?

TEKS Number and Operations—K.3.C
MATHEMATICAL PROCESSES
K.1.B, K.1.D

14.4 PROBLEM SOLVING • Subtraction Word Problems

? Essential Question How can you solve subtraction word problems and complete the subtraction sentence?

Unlock the Problem Real World

DIRECTIONS Listen to the subtraction word problem about the squirrels. Circle and mark an X on the squirrels that are leaving. How many squirrels are left in the tree? Write and trace the subtraction sentence.

Try Another Problem

1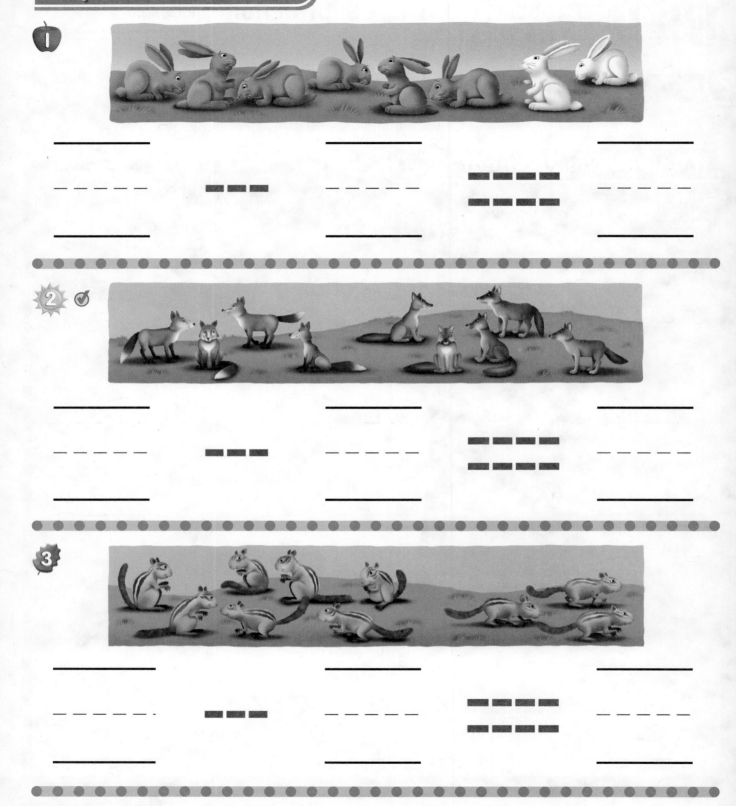

_____   _____   _____

- - - - - - -   ▬ ▬ ▬   - - - - -   ▬ ▬ ▬   - - - - -
                                              ▬ ▬ ▬

_____   _____   _____

⎯⎯⎯⎯⎯⎯⎯⎯⎯⎯⎯⎯⎯⎯⎯⎯⎯⎯⎯⎯⎯⎯⎯

2 ✓

_____   _____   _____

- - - - - - -   ▬ ▬ ▬   - - - - -   ▬ ▬ ▬   - - - - -
                                              ▬ ▬ ▬

_____   _____   _____

⎯⎯⎯⎯⎯⎯⎯⎯⎯⎯⎯⎯⎯⎯⎯⎯⎯⎯⎯⎯⎯⎯⎯

3

_____   _____

- - - - - - -   ▬ ▬ ▬   - - - - -   ▬ ▬ ▬   - - - - -
                                              ▬ ▬ ▬

_____   _____

⎯⎯⎯⎯⎯⎯⎯⎯⎯⎯⎯⎯⎯⎯⎯⎯⎯⎯⎯⎯⎯⎯⎯

DIRECTIONS **1–2.** Listen to the subtraction word problem. Write and trace to complete the subtraction sentence. **3.** Listen to the subtraction word problem. Circle and mark an X on the chipmunks that run away. Write and trace to complete the subtraction sentence.

Name _____

4

_____ ▬▬▬ _____ ▬▬▬▬ _ _ _ _

_____ _ _ _ _____ ▬▬▬▬ _____

5

_____ ▬▬▬ _____ ▬▬▬▬ _ _ _ _

_____ _ _ _ _____ ▬▬▬▬ _____

6

_ _ _ _ ▬▬▬ _ _ _ ▬▬▬▬ _ _ _ _

_____ _____ _____ ▬▬▬▬ _____

DIRECTIONS **4–5.** Listen to the subtraction word problem. Circle and mark an X on the animals that leave. Write and trace to complete the subtraction sentence. **6.** Listen to the subtraction word problem. Write and trace to complete the subtraction sentence.

HOME ACTIVITY • Tell your child a subtraction word problem. Have your child write a subtraction sentence to match the story.

7

○ **5 − 3 = 2**

○ **8 − 5 = 3**

8

○ **4**

○ **5**

9

○ **10**

○ **2**

DIRECTIONS Choose the correct answer. **7.** There are 8 birds. Five of the birds are yellow. The rest of the birds are red. Which number sentence shows how to find the number of red birds? **8.** There are 7 raccoons. Three of the raccoons walk away. How many raccoons are left? **9.** There are 10 frogs. Some of the frogs hop away. Now there are 8 frogs left. How many frogs hopped away?

TEKS Number and Operations—K.3.C
MATHEMATICAL PROCESSES K.1.B, K.1.D

Name _____

14.4 PROBLEM SOLVING
• Subtraction Word Problems

1

_____

- - - - - 　 ▬ ▬ 　 - - - - - 　 ▬ ▬ ▬ 　 - - - - -
　　　　　　　　　　　　　　　　 ▬ ▬ ▬

_____

2

_____

- - - - - 　 ▬ ▬ ▬ 　 - - - - - 　 ▬ ▬ 　 - - - - -
　　　　　　　　　　　　　　　　 ▬ ▬ ▬

_____

DIRECTIONS Write and trace to complete the subtraction sentence. **1.** There are six bears. Two bears run away. Circle and mark an X on the bears that leave. **2.** There are ten turkeys. Seven turkeys run away. Circle and mark an X on the turkeys that leave.

3

○ $5 - 2 = 3$

ⓓ $7 - 2 = 5$

4

ⓐ **5**

ⓑ **9**

5

○ **4**

○ **3**

DIRECTIONS Choose the correct answer.
3. There are 7 cats. Two of them run away. What is $7 - 2$? **4.** There are 9 beavers. Four of them swim away. What is $9 - 4$? **5.** There are 6 eagles. Three fly away. What is $6 - 3$?

Name _____

Concepts and Skills

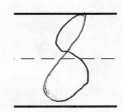

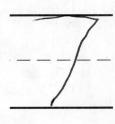

DIRECTIONS **I.** Count the pennies. Write the number that shows how many pennies. ↳ TEKS K.4 **2.** Count the nickels. Write the number that shows how many nickels. ↳ TEKS K.4 **3.** Count the dimes. Write the number that shows how many dimes. ↳ TEKS K.4

4

_____
- - - - - -
_____

5

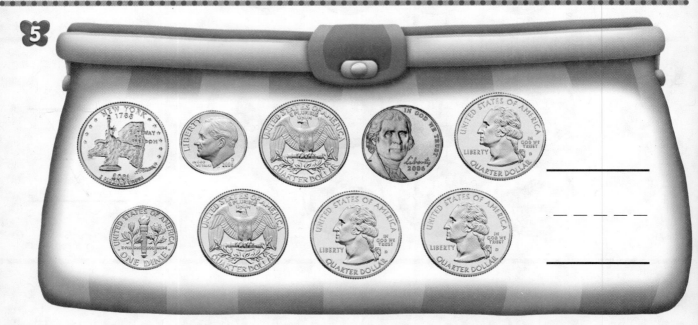

_____
- - - - - -
_____

6 ⭐ **TEXAS Test Prep**

    ○   ○

DIRECTIONS   **4.** Circle the nickels. Count and write the number of nickels. ⬥ TEKS K.4   **5.** Circle the quarters. Count and write the number of quarters. ⬥ TEKS K.4   **6.** Choose the correct answer. Suzi needs 2 dimes to buy a snack. Which set shows the coins Suzi needs? ⬥ TEKS K.4

Name _____

 ✓ **Unit 2 Assessment**

Vocabulary

 1

_____
- - - - - - - - - -
_____

add

 2

_____
- - - - - - - - - -
_____

subtract

Concepts and Skills

 3

_____   _____   _____
- - - - - - - -   ▬ ▬   - - - - - - - -   ▬▬▬▬   - - - - - - -
_____   ▬▬▬▬

DIRECTIONS **I.** Write the number of each color cubes. Write the number to show how many in all. ▶ TEKS K.3.A   **2.** Write the number to show how many are left. ▶ TEKS K.3.A   **3.** Draw blue cubes to make a nine-cube train. Three cubes are yellow and the rest are blue. Write to complete the subtraction sentence. ▶ TEKS K.3.B

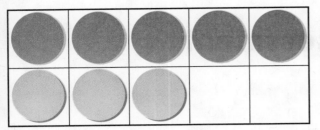

$$4 + 4 \qquad 5 + 3$$
○   ○

5

$$2 + 2 = 4 \qquad 3 + 1 = 4$$
○   ○

6

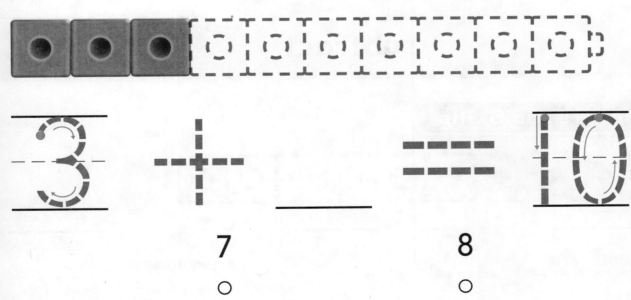

7   8
○   ○

DIRECTIONS **4.** Mark under the addition that shows the sets put together.
TEKS K.3.A **5.** Mark under the addition sentence that shows how many there are
when the cubes are put together. TEKS K.3.A **6.** How many red cubes do you see?
How many blue cubes do you need to add to make 10? Use blue to color those cubes.
Mark under the number that would complete the addition sentence. TEKS K.3.B

$$8 - \underline{\quad} = 6$$

	2
○	○

○ 7

○ 4

○ 9

○ 5

DIRECTIONS **7.** Mark under the number that shows how many birds are being taken from the set. ⬥ TEKS K.3.C **8.** Mark beside the number that shows how many quarters are in this group. ⬥ TEKS K.4 **9.** Mark beside the number that shows how many nickels are in this group. ⬥ TEKS K.4

Performance Task

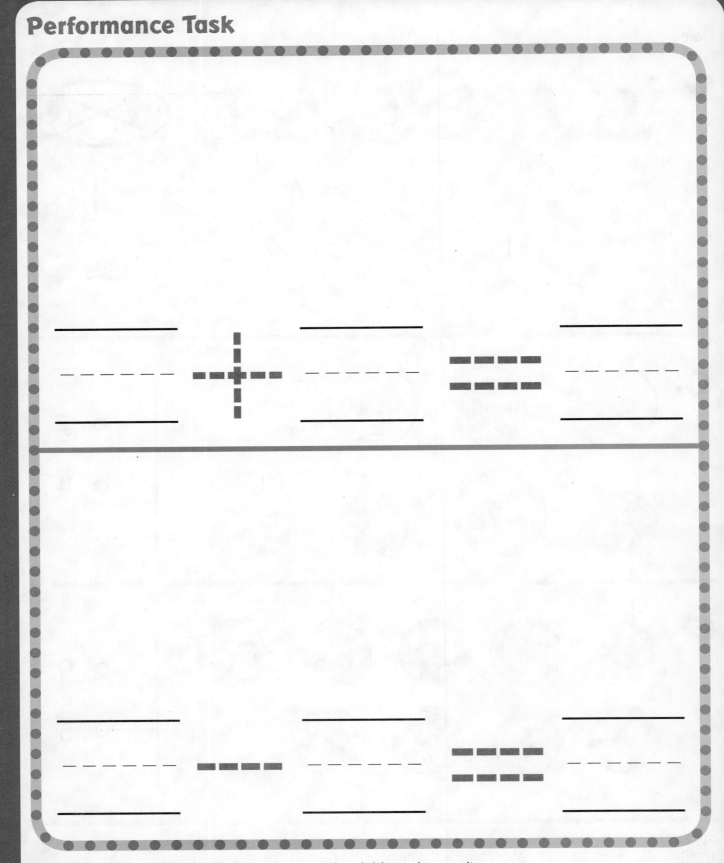

PERFORMANCE TASK This task will assess the child's understanding
of addition and subtraction. TEKS K.3.A, K.3.B, K.3.C

Algebraic Reasoning

Name _____

17 and 18

 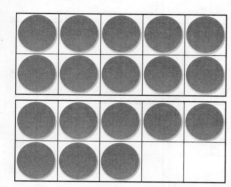

_____

- - - - - - - - -

_____

 17

19 and 20

 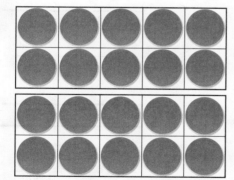

_____

- - - - - - - - -

_____

DIRECTIONS 1. Count how many. Write the number. **2.** Look at the number. Draw that number of balls. **3.** Count how many. Write the number.

FAMILY NOTE: This page checks your child's understanding of important skills needed for success in Unit 3.

 GO DIGITAL Assessment Options: Soar to Success Math

Visualize It

one

ten

twenty

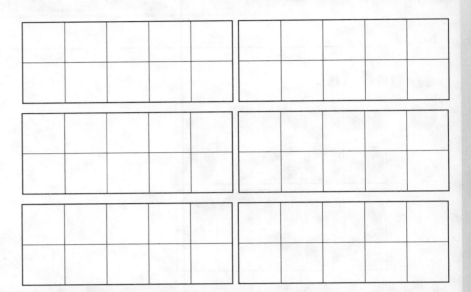

Understand Vocabulary

DIRECTIONS **Visualize It** Read the number. Draw counters to show the number.

Understand Vocabulary Trace the number word. Write the number.

GO DIGITAL • Interactive Student Edition • Multimedia eGlossary

Collection Day

written by Chloe Weasley

This Take-Home Book belongs to

_____

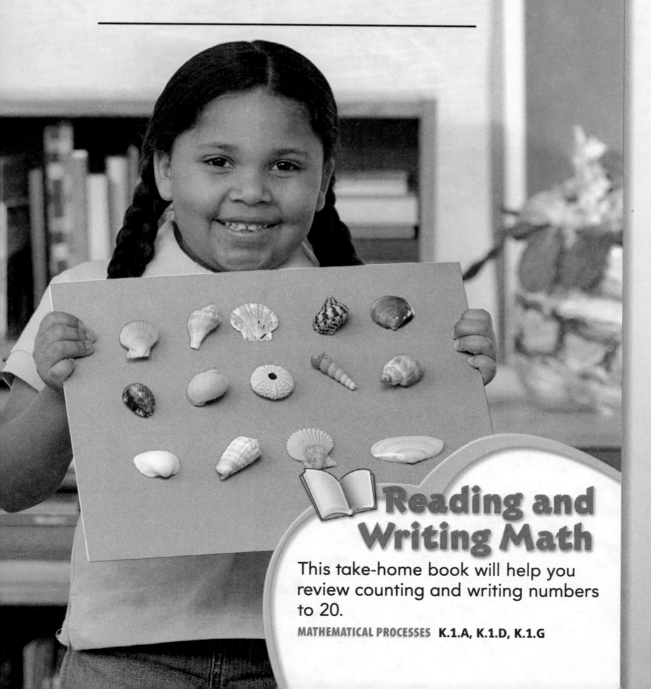

Reading and Writing Math

This take-home book will help you review counting and writing numbers to 20.

MATHEMATICAL PROCESSES   K.1.A, K.1.D, K.1.G

The day had come, their collections they brought.
Things that they had made, had found, or had bought.

Brian brought marbles, big ones and small.
How many marbles did he bring in all?

Sarah brought rocks, some pretty, some gray.

How many in all did she show friends today?

Kathy brought wind-up toys that can walk.

Some were noisy, and one even squawked.

How many in all did Kathy bring?

Sean brought in his collection of
dinosaurs. Have you seen?
Count to see if he brought more
or less than nineteen.

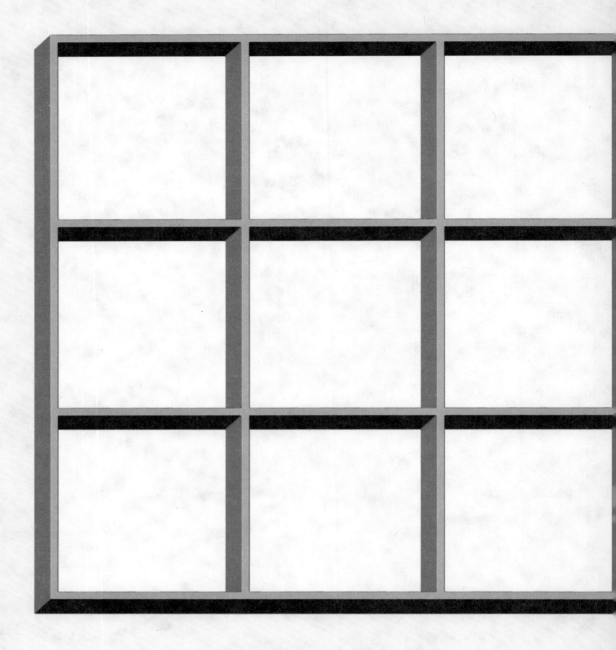

Imagine that you bring a collection of things to school. What would you like to bring? Draw your collection.

Name _____

DIRECTIONS Look at the box and the collection of shells. Draw more shells. Tell a friend a story about the shell collection.

How Many in All?

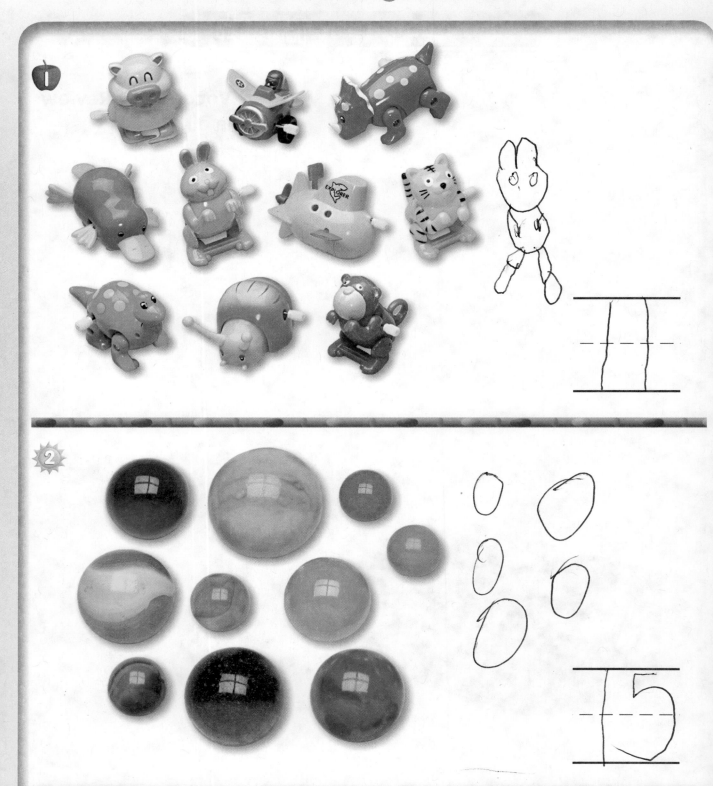

DIRECTIONS **I.** Count the toys. Then draw more toys. Write how many in all. **2.** Count the marbles. Then draw more marbles. Write how many in all.

542

Name _____

16.1 Count to 50 by Ones

? Essential Question

How does the order of numbers help you count to 50 by ones?

Explore

1	2	3	4	5	6	7	8	9	10
11	12	13	14	15	16	17	18	19	20
21	22	23	24	25	26	27	28	29	30
31	32	33	34	35	36	37	38	39	40
41	42	43	44	45	46	47	48	49	(50)

DIRECTIONS Point to each number as you count to 50. Trace the circle around the number 50.

1	2	3	4	5	6	7	8	9	10
11	12	13	14	15	16	17	18	19	20
21	22	23	24	25	26	27	28	29	30
31	32	33	34	35	36	37	38	39	40
41	42	43	44	45	46	47	48	49	50

DIRECTIONS **1.** Point to each number as you count to 50. Draw a line under the number 50. Circle the number 15. Begin with 15 and count forward to 50 again. Color the box with the number 39 yellow. Begin with 39 and count forward to 50 again. Mark an X on the number 20. Count backward from 20 to 1.

16.1 Count to 50 by Ones

1	2	3	4	5	6	7	8	9	10
11	12	13	14	15	16	17	18	19	20
21	22	23	24	25	26	27	28	29	30
31	32	33	34	35	36	37	38	39	40
41	42	43	44	45	46	47	48	49	50

DIRECTIONS I. Point to each number as you count to 50. Draw a line under the number 50. Circle the number 22. Begin with 22 and count forward to 50. Find the number 36. Color the box with the number 36 yellow. Begin with 36 and count forward to 50. Mark an X on the number right after 42. Count forward from that number to 50.

2

11	12	13	14		16	17	18	19	20
21	22	23	24	25	26	27	28	29	30

∅ **15**

○ **25**

3

21	22	23	24	25	26	27	28	29	30
31	32	33	34	35	36	37		39	40

○ **28**

⊘ **38**

DIRECTIONS Choose the correct answer.
2–3. Point to each number as you count.
What is the missing number?

51	52	53	54	55	56	57	58	59	60
61	62	63	64	65	66	67	68	69	70
71	72	73	74	75	76	77	78	79	80
81	82	83	84	85	86	87	88	89	90
91	92	93	94	95	96	97	98	99	100

DIRECTIONS **2.** Trace the numbers to complete the counting order to 100. Count by tens as you point to the numbers you traced.

HOME ACTIVITY • Show your child a calendar. Use self-stick notes to cover random numbers. Ask your child to say the numbers that are covered. Then have him or her remove the self-stick notes to check.

Problem Solving

1	2	3	4	5	6	7	8	9	10
11	12	13	14	15	16	17	18	19	— — —
21	22	23	24	25	26	27	28	29	30

Daily Assessment Task

10	20	30	40	50	60	70	80		100

○ **70**   ○ **90**

DIRECTIONS **3.** Listen to the problem. What is the last number Jenny says? Write the number. What is the last number that Lindsay will say? Draw a line under the number. **4.** Choose the correct answer. When you count by tens, what number comes after 80?

558 five hundred fifty-eight

TEKS Algebraic Reasoning—K.5
Also K.2.A, K.2.C
MATHEMATICAL PROCESSES K.1.F

Name _____

16.3 Count to 100 by Tens

1

1	2	3	4	5	6	7	8	9	____
11	12	13	14	15	16	17	18	19	____
21	22	23	24	25	26	27	28	29	____
31	32	33	34	35	36	37	38	39	____
41	42	43	44	45	46	47	48	49	____

DIRECTIONS **1.** Write the numbers to complete the counting order to 50. Count by tens as you point to the numbers you wrote.

Module 16

five hundred fifty-nine **559**

2

10	20	30	40		60	70	80	90	100

○ **30**   ○ **50**

3

10	20	30	40	50	60	70		90	100

○ **80**   ○ **60**

4

10	20		40	50	60	70	80	90	100

○ **10**   ○ **30**

DIRECTIONS Choose the correct answer.
2. When you count by tens, what number comes after 40?
3. When you count by tens, what number comes after 70?
4. When you count by tens, what number comes after 20?

Name _____

16.4 PROBLEM SOLVING • Count from Any Number

Essential Question
How can you solve problems using logical reasoning?

Unlock the Problem

1	2	3	4	5	6	7	8	9	10
11	12	13	14	15	16	17	18	19	20
21	22	23	24	25	26	27	28	29	30
31	32	33	34	35	36	37	38	39	40
41	42	43	44	45	46	47	48	49	50

DIRECTIONS Listen to each number riddle. Use the fifty chart and the clues to solve each riddle. Count from the secret number to 50.

1	2	3	4	5	6	7	8	9	10
11	12	13	14	15	16	17	18	19	20
21	22	23	24	25	26	27	28	29	30
31	32	33	34	35	36	37	38	39	40
41	42	43	44	45	46	47	48	49	50
51	52	53	54	55	56	57	58	59	60
61	62	63	64	65	66	67	68	69	70
71	72	73	74	75	76	77	78	79	80
81	82	83	84	85	86	87	88	89	90
91	92	93	94	95	96	97	98	99	100

DIRECTIONS **1.** Listen to each number riddle. Use the hundred chart and the clues to solve each riddle. Count from the secret number to 100.

Name _____

1	2	3	4	5	6	7	8	9	10
11	12	13	14	15	16	17	18	19	20
21	22	23	24	25	26	27	28	29	30
31	32	33	34	35	36	37	38	39	40
41	42	43	44	45	46	47	48	49	50
51	52	53	54	55	56	57	58	59	60
61	62	63	64	65	66	67	68	69	70
71	72	73	74	75	76	77	78	79	80
81	82	83	84	85	86	87	88	89	90
91	92	93	94	95	96	97	98	99	100

DIRECTIONS **2.** Listen to each number riddle. Use the hundred chart and the clues to solve each riddle. Count from the secret number to 100.

HOME ACTIVITY • Give your child a hundred chart. Say a number riddle. For example, *I am greater than 40. I am less than 42. What number am I?* Have your child circle the number on the chart.

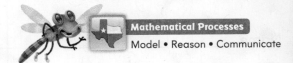
3

| 41 | 42 | 43 | 44 | 45 | 46 | 47 | 48 | | 50 |

○ **48**   ○ **49**

4

| 50 | 60 | 70 | | 90 | 100 |

○ **70**   ○ **80**

5

| 61 | 62 | 63 | 64 | 65 | 66 | 67 | 68 | 69 | 70 |
| 71 | 72 | 73 | 74 | 75 | 76 | 77 | 78 | 79 | 80 |

○ **69, 70, 71**

○ **67, 68, 69**

DIRECTIONS Choose the correct answer. **3.** Point to each number as you count. What is the missing number? **4.** Count by tens. What is the missing number? **5.** Which three numbers come after 68?

564 five hundred sixty-four

16.4 PROBLEM SOLVING • Count from Any Number

1	2	3	4	5	6	7	8	9	10
11	12	13	14	15	16	17	18	19	20
21	22	23	24	25	26	27	28	29	30
31	32	33	34	35	36	37	38	39	40
41	42	43	44	45	46	47	48	49	50
51	52	53	54	55	56	57	58	59	60
61	62	63	64	65	66	67	68	69	70
71	72	73	74	75	76	77	78	79	80
81	82	83	84	85	86	87	88	89	90
91	92	93	94	95	96	97	98	99	100

DIRECTIONS   1. Solve the number riddles.
Riddle 1: I am between 41 and 50. I am one more
than 45. What number am I? Circle the number.
Count from this number to 100. **Riddle 2:** You say
my number when you count by tens. I am greater
than 50. I am less than 70. What number am I?
Color the box with my number red. Count from
this number to 100.

②

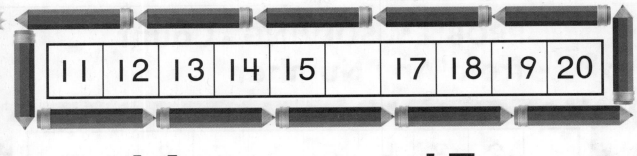

| 11 | 12 | 13 | 14 | 15 | | 17 | 18 | 19 | 20 |

○ **16**   ○ **15**

③

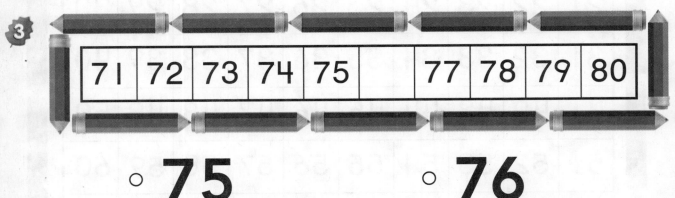

| 71 | 72 | 73 | 74 | 75 | | 77 | 78 | 79 | 80 |

○ **75**   ○ **76**

④

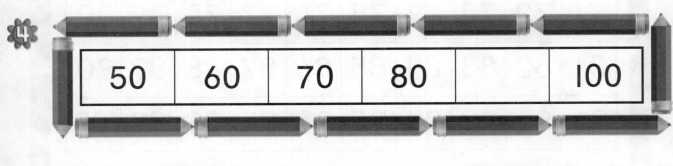

| 50 | 60 | 70 | 80 | | 100 |

○ **90**   ○ **50**

DIRECTIONS Choose the correct answer.
2–3. Point to each number as you count. What is the missing number? **4.** Count by tens. What is the missing number?

Name _____

Vocabulary

 1   40   50   60

2   1   51   100

Concepts and Skills

3

1	2	3	4	5	6	7	8	9	10
11	12	13	14	15	16	17	18	19	20
21	22	23	24	25	26	27	28	29	30
31	32	33	34	35	36	37	38	39	40
41	42	43	44	45	46	47	48	49	50

4

1	2	3	4	5	6	7	8	9	10
11	12	13	14	15	16	17	18	19	20
21	22	23	24	25	26	27	28	29	30
31	32	33	34	35	36	37	38	39	40
41	42	43	44	45	46	47	48	49	50

DIRECTIONS 1. Circle the number fifty. **2.** Circle the number one hundred.
3. Circle the number 34. Begin with 34 and count forward to 50. Underline the
number 50. ↘ TEKS K.5   **4.** What number is one more than 39? Circle that number.
Begin with that number and count forward to 50. ↘ TEKS K.5

1	2	3	4	5	6	7	8	9	10
11	12	13	14	15	16	17	18	19	20
21	22	23	24	25	26	27	28	29	30
31	32	33	34	35	36	37	38	39	40
41	42	43	44	45	46	47	48	49	50
51	52	53	54	55	56	57	58	59	60
61	62	63	64	65	66	67	68	69	70
71	72	73	74	75	76	77	78	79	80
81	82	83	84	85	86	87	88	89	90
91	92	93	94	95	96	97	98		100

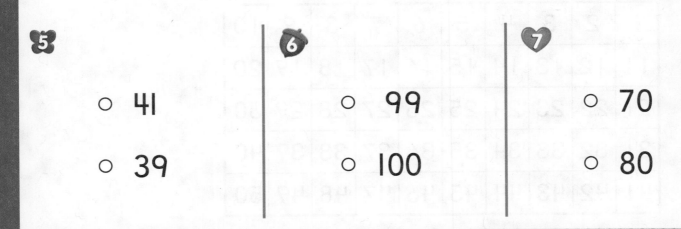

5

○ 41

○ 39

6

○ 99

○ 100

7

○ 70

○ 80

DIRECTIONS Fill in the circle for the correct answer choice. **5.** Look at the hundred chart. What number is one less than 40? TEKS K.5 **6.** Look at the hundred chart. What number is missing? TEKS K.5 **7.** Look at the column highlighted in yellow on the hundred chart. When counting by tens, what number comes right after 60? TEKS K.5

| 10 | 20 | | 40 | 50 | 60 | 70 | 80 | 90 | 100 |

10   30
○   ○

1	2	3	4	5	6	7	8	9	10
11	12	13	14	15	16	17	18	19	20
21	22	23	24	25	26	27	28	29	30
31	32	33	34	35	36	37	38	39	40
41	42	43	44	45	46	47	48	49	50
51	52	53	54	55	56	57	58	59	60
61	62	63	64	65	66	67	68	69	70
71	72	73	74	75	76	77	78	79	80
81	82	83	84	85	86	87	88	89	90
91	92	93	94	95	96	97	98	99	100

○ 52, 53, 54

○ 58, 59, 60

○ 90, 91, 92

○ 86, 87, 88

DIRECTIONS Fill in the circle for the correct answer choice. **8.** Count by tens.
What is the missing number? TEKS K.5 **9.** Look at the hundred chart. Which three
numbers come after 57? TEKS K.5 **10.** Look at the hundred chart. Which three
numbers come after 89? TEKS K.5

Performance Task

| 18 | 20 | 19 | 17 |

_____ _____ _____ _____

- -

_____ _____ _____ _____

| 41 | 42 | 43 | 44 | 45 | 46 | 47 | 48 | 49 | 50 |

| 51 | 52 | 54 | 53 | 55 | 56 | 57 | 58 | 59 | 60 |

| 61 | 62 | 63 | 64 | 65 | 66 | 67 | 68 | 69 | 70 |

PERFORMANCE TASK This task will assess the child's understanding of identifying and counting numbers to 100.

Geometry and Measurement

Show What You Know

Name _____

Alike and Different

 1

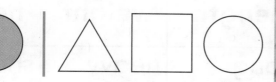

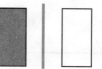 **2**

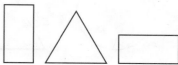

Bigger and Smaller

 3

 4

DIRECTIONS **1.** Look at the shape at the beginning of the row. Color the shape that is alike. **2.** Look at the shape at the beginning of the row. Color the shape that is different. **3.** Mark an X on the dog that is smaller. **4.** Mark an X on the tree that is bigger.

 FAMILY NOTE: This page checks your child's understanding of important skills needed for success in Unit 4.

Vocabulary Builder

Review Words

circle	shorter
square	taller
triangle	heavier
rectangle	lighter
longer	

Visualize

1

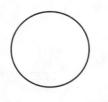

2

length	weight	height
long	heavy	short
longer	heavier	shorter
short		tall
shorter		taller

Understand Vocabulary

3

4

5

DIRECTIONS **Visualize It 1.** Look at the shapes. Color the circle red. Color the square yellow. Color the triangle blue. Color the rectangle purple. **2.** Circle the review words that are the same for two different kinds of measurement.

Understand Vocabulary 3. Circle the pencil that is longer. **4.** Circle the tree that is taller. **5.** Circle the object that is heavier.

GO DIGITAL
- Interactive Student Edition
- Multimedia eGlossary

Vocabulary Reader

Grandma's Rooftop Garden

written by J. D. McDonnell

illustrated by Viviana Garofoli

This Take-Home Book belongs to

____

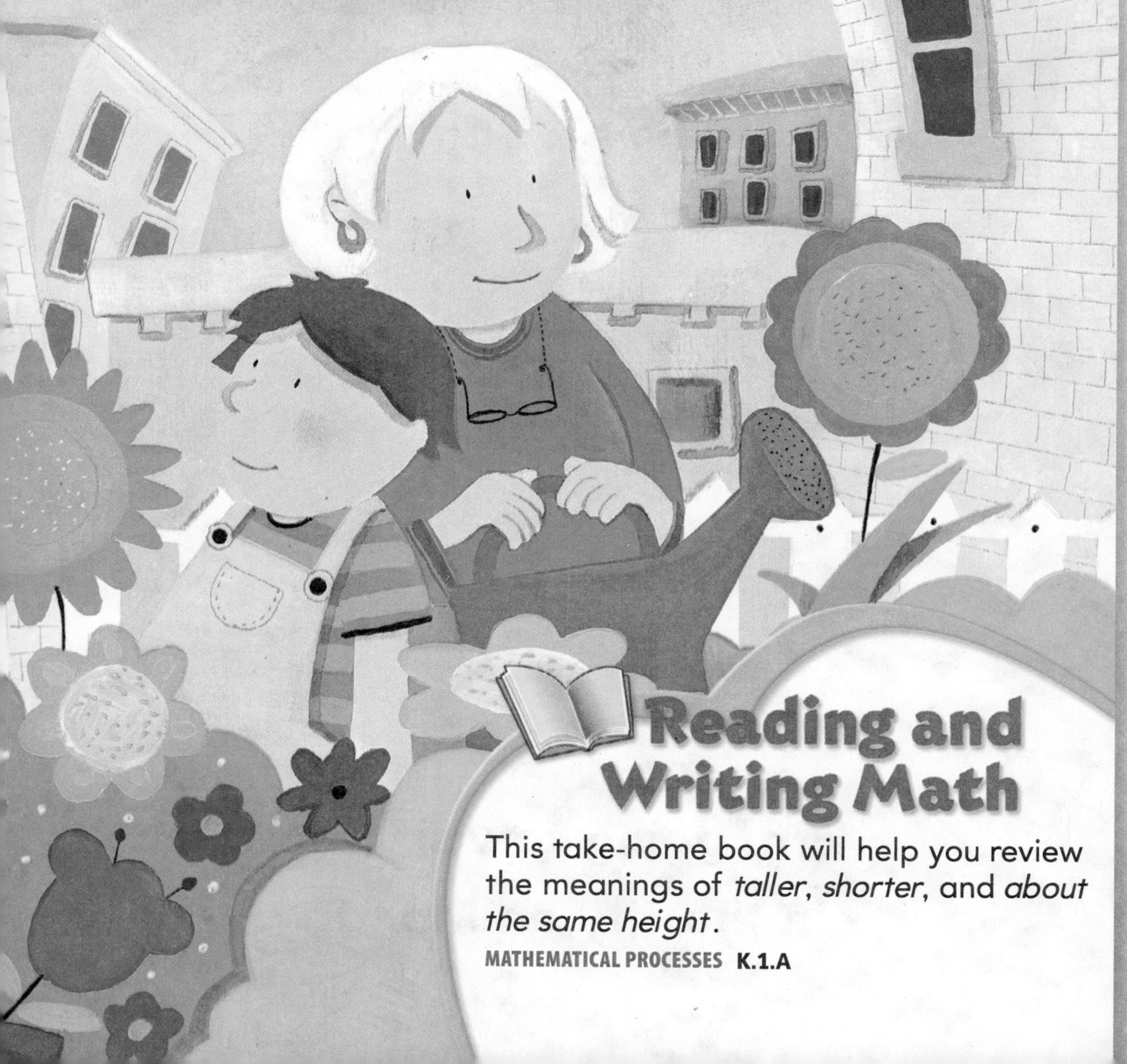

Reading and Writing Math

This take-home book will help you review the meanings of *taller*, *shorter*, and *about the same height*.

MATHEMATICAL PROCESSES K.1.A

I'm going to visit Grandma
in the city on Monday.

My grandmother lives in the tallest
building on the block. Can you find
her building? Can you find which is
the shortest building on the block?

Grandma has a garden on
the rooftop of her building!
The last time I came to visit,
we planted seeds.

After we planted seeds,
flowers started to grow.
Now look how much the
flowers have grown!

I pick a flower. Then Grandma picks
a flower. Which flower is shorter?

Circle Grandma's tallest tomato plant.
Cross out her shortest tomato plant.

Can you help Grandma's garden grow? Draw a taller flower. Draw a shorter flower.

Name _____

Vocabulary Review
short
tall

DIRECTIONS Look at the building and street. Draw a tall building and a short building. Draw a tall person and a short person. Tell a story about the city block. Ask a friend to tell which buildings and people are tall and which are short.

581

Short or Tall?

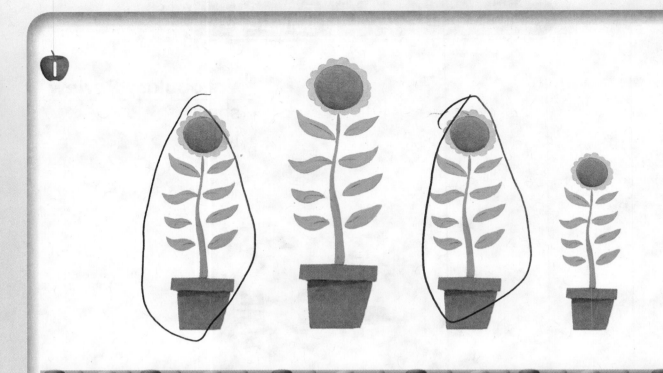

DIRECTIONS **I.** Look at the plants. Circle the two plants that are about the same height. **2.** Look at the flowers. Draw another flower. Make it taller than the pink flower. Make it shorter than the yellow flower.

582

Name ______________________________

17.5 HANDS ON

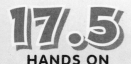

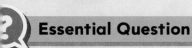

PROBLEM SOLVING • Create Shapes

TEKS Geometry and Measurement—K.6.F, K.6.A
MATHEMATICAL PROCESSES K.1.C

Essential Question How can you solve problems using the strategy draw a picture?

Unlock the Problem

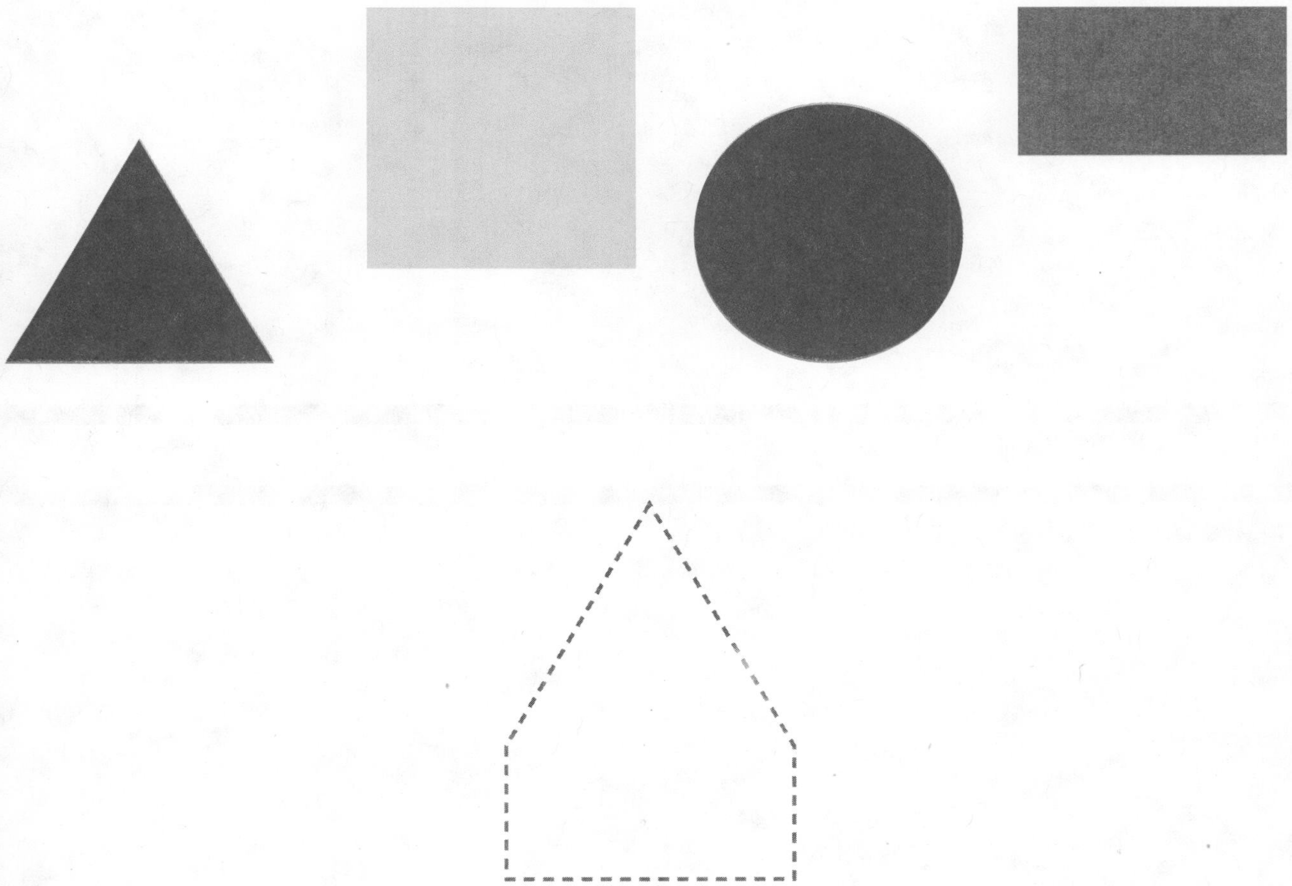

DIRECTIONS Which shapes can be joined to make the larger shape? Circle the shapes. Trace and color to show the shapes that you used.

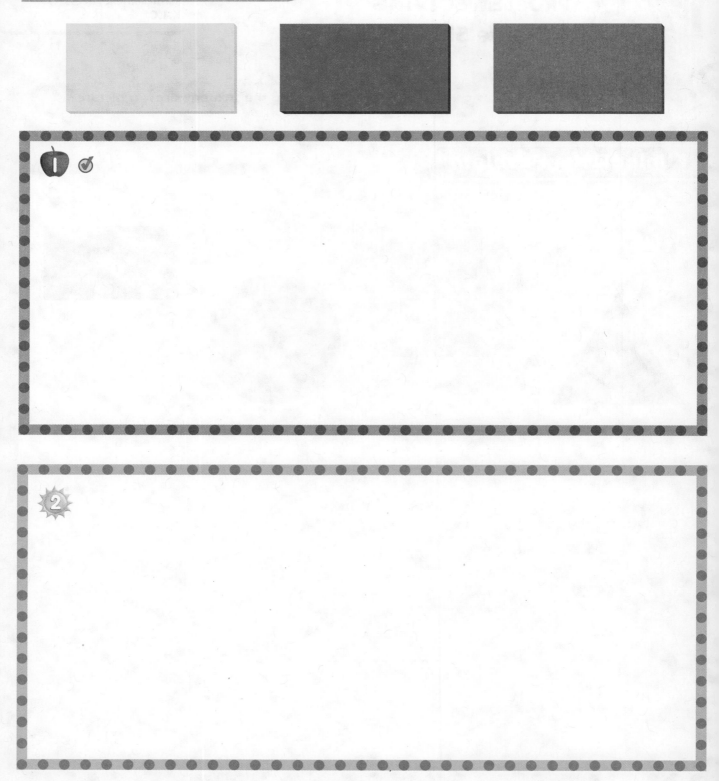

DIRECTIONS **I.** How can you join some of the small rectangles to make a square? Use the rectangle shapes to make a square. Draw the square you make. **2.** How can you join some rectangles to make a large rectangle that is not a square? Use the rectangle shapes to make a large rectangle. Draw the rectangle you make.

Name _____

3

4

DIRECTIONS **3.** Use rectangles and triangles from the two-dimensional shapes to make a crown. Draw the crown you make. **4.** Use 3 different two-dimensional shapes. Join them together to make a new shape. Trace and draw the shape you make.

HOME ACTIVITY • Have your child join shapes to form a larger shape, and then tell you about the shape.

5

○   ○

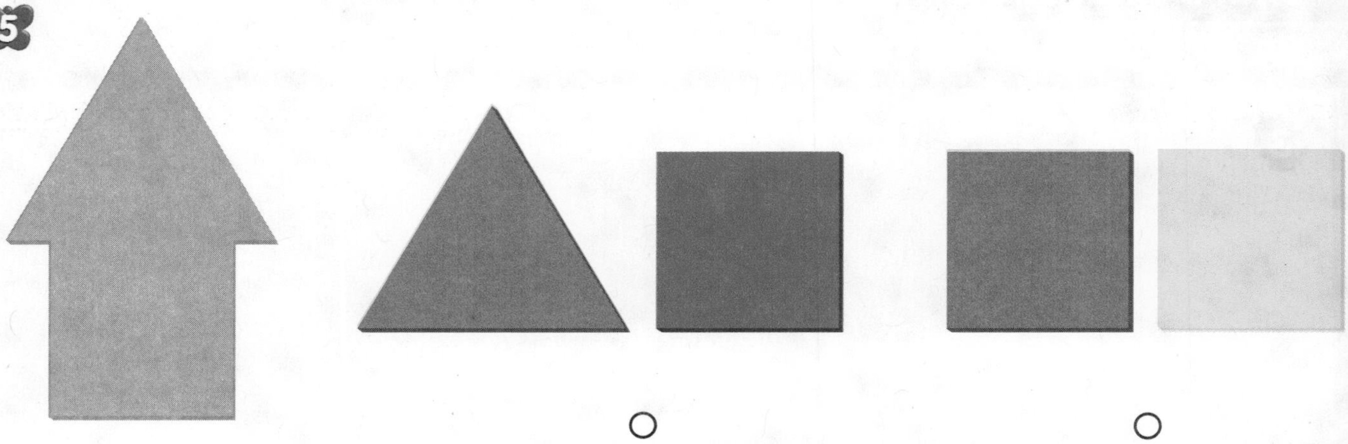

6

○   ○

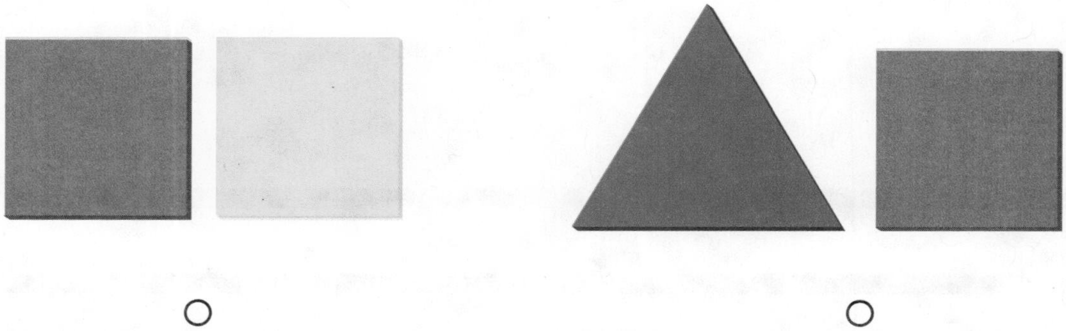

7

○   ○

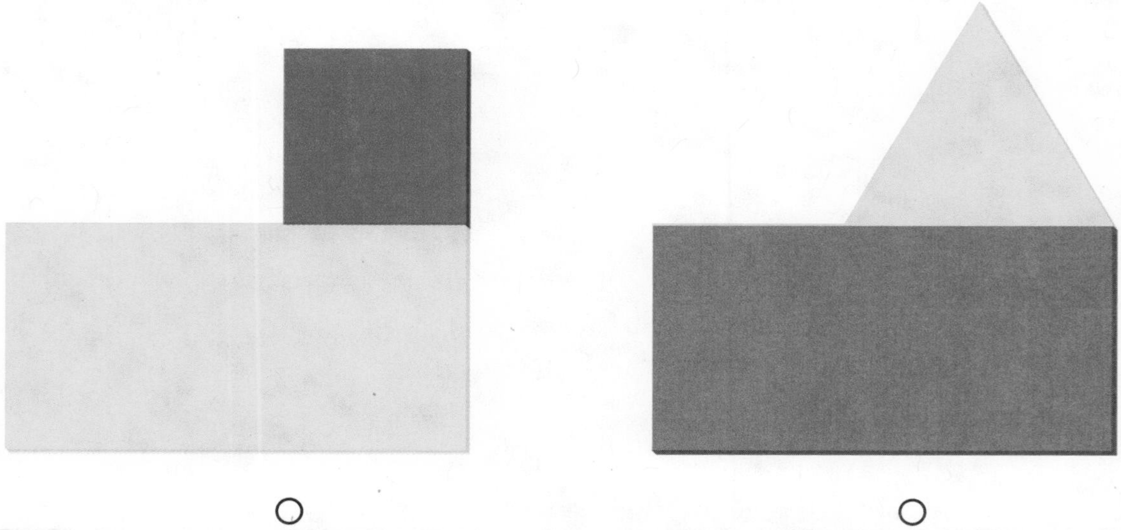

DIRECTIONS Choose the correct answer. **5.** Which two shapes were used to make the gray shape? **6.** Jackson uses two shapes to make a rectangle. Which two shapes does he use? **7.** Which shows a shape made by joining two rectangles?

610 six hundred ten

TEKS Geometry and Measurement—K.6.F
Also K.6.A
MATHEMATICAL PROCESSES K.1.C

17.5 PROBLEM SOLVING • Create Shapes
HANDS ON

1

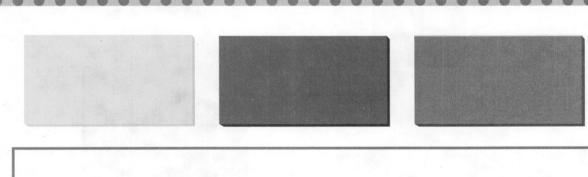

2

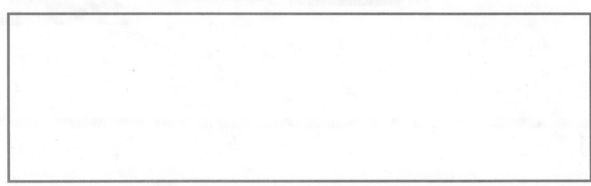

DIRECTIONS **1.** How can you join the two squares to make a rectangle? Draw the rectangle.
2. How can you join some rectangles to make a larger rectangle? Draw the rectangle you make.

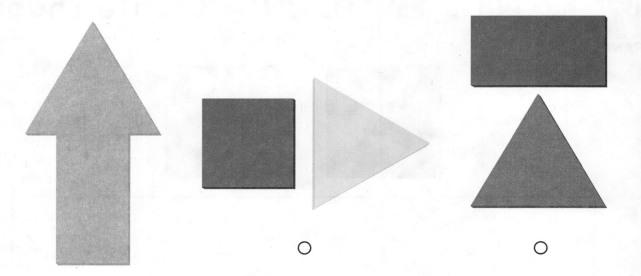

○   ○

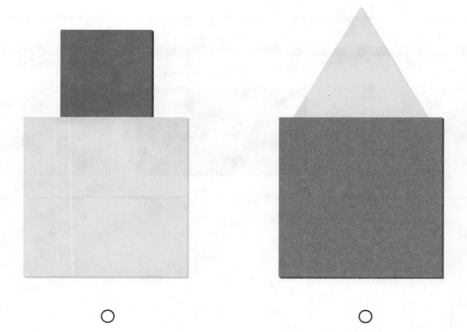

○   ○

DIRECTIONS Choose the correct answer.
3. Which two shapes were used to make the gray shape? **4.** Jeff makes a shape by joining a square and a triangle. Which shape does Jeff make?

Module 17 Assessment

Concepts and Skills

 1

_____

- - - - - - -

_____ **sides**

_____

- - - - - - -

_____ **vertices**

 2

_____

- - - - - - -

_____ **sides**

_____

- - - - - - -

_____ **vertices**

 3

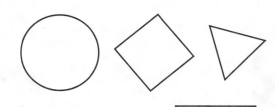

4

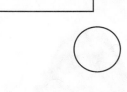
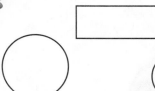

DIRECTIONS **1–2.** Trace around each shape. Write how many sides. Place a counter on each corner or vertex. Write how many vertices. ✦ TEKS K.6.D **3.** Color all of the circles. ✦ TEKS K.6.A **4.** Color all of the triangles. ✦ TEKS K.6.A

5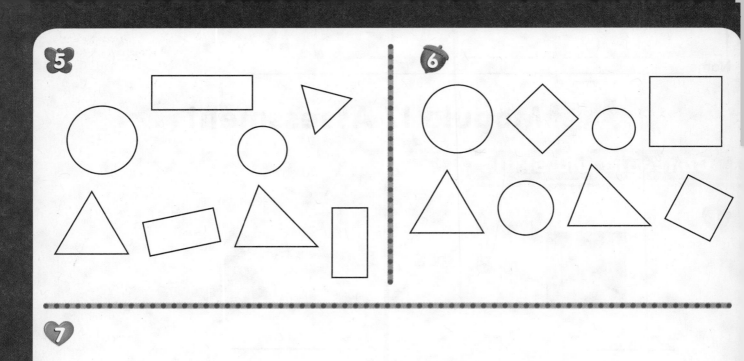

6

7

8 ⭐ **TEXAS Test Prep**

   ○   ○   ○

DIRECTIONS **5.** Color all of the rectangles. ⬇ TEKS K.6.A **6.** Color all of the squares. ⬇ TEKS K.6.A **7.** Use 3 small squares to make a rectangle. Draw and color the shapes you use. ⬇ TEKS K.6.F **8.** Mark under the shape that is a triangle. ⬇ TEKS K.6.A, K.6.D

TEKS Geometry and Measurement—K.7.A

MATHEMATICAL PROCESSES
K.1.B

19.1 PROBLEM SOLVING • Measuring an Object

Essential Question How can you solve problems by drawing a picture?

Explore

DIRECTIONS Katie wants to measure the jar. What can she find out?

Share and Show

1

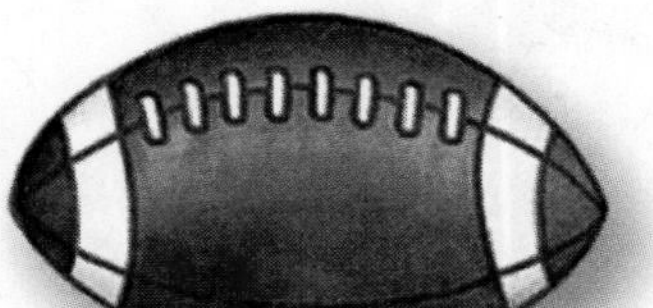

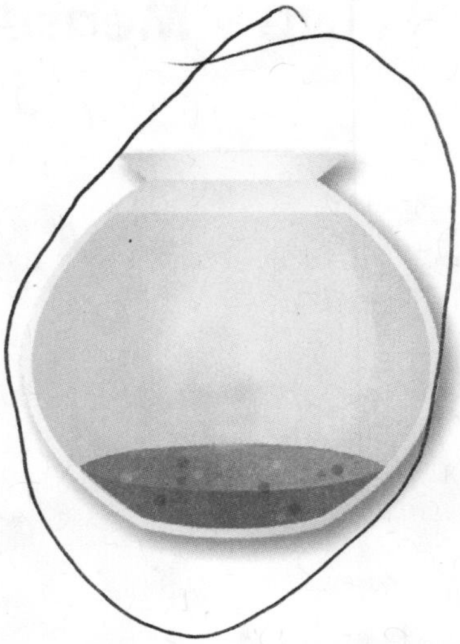

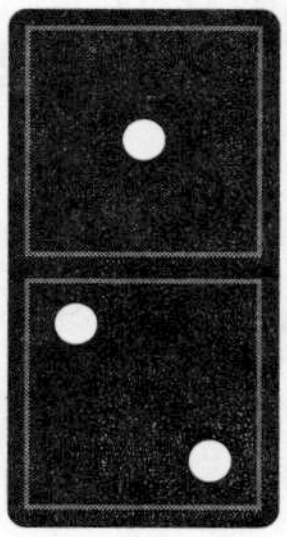

2

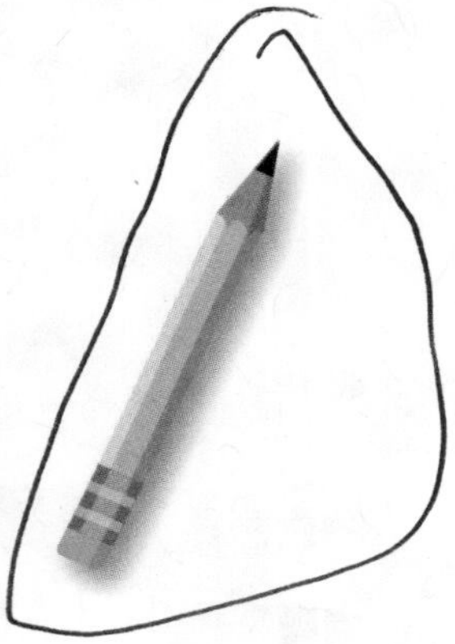

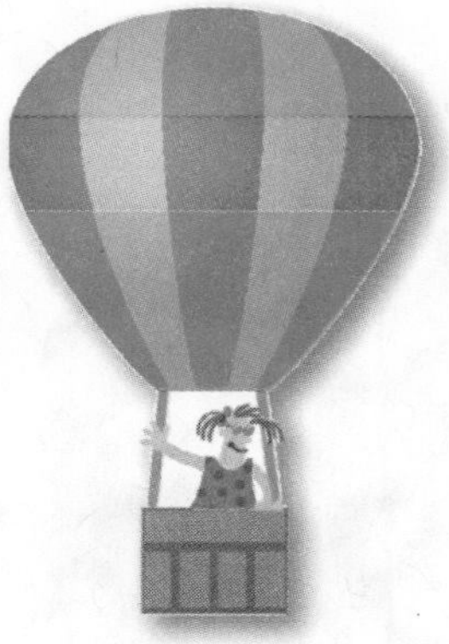

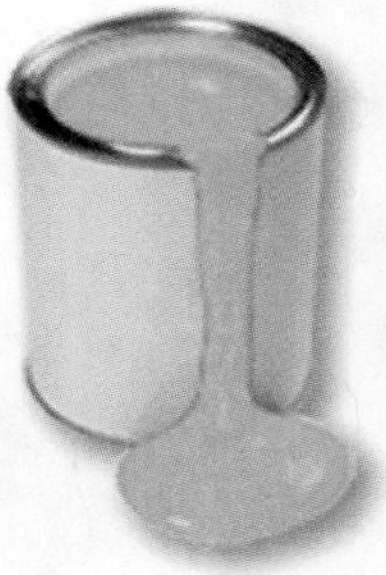

3

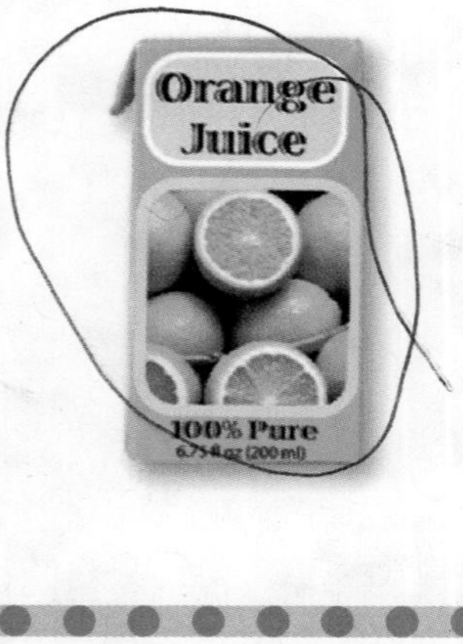

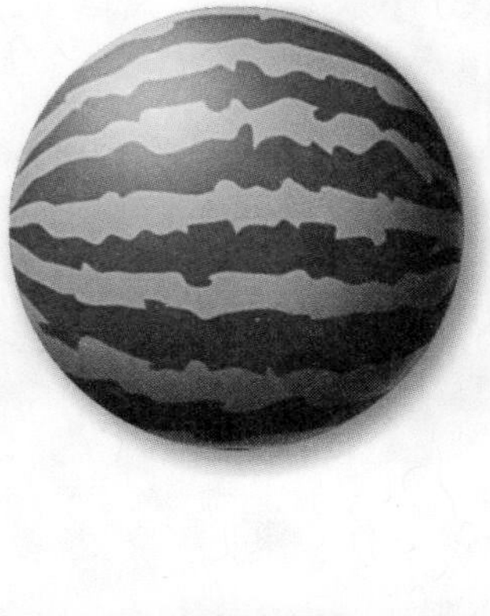

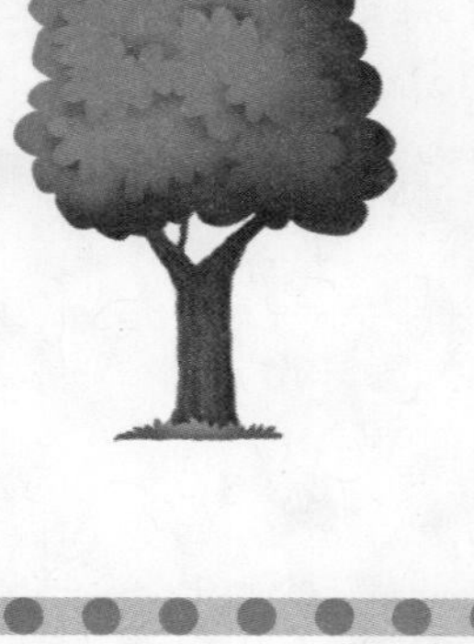

DIRECTIONS **1.** Which object would you most likely measure to find out how much it holds? Circle the object. **2.** Which object would you most likely measure to find out how long it is? Circle the object. **3.** Which object would you most likely measure to find out how much it weighs? Circle the object.

4

5

6

DIRECTIONS **4.** Draw an object that you would measure to find its weight. **5.** Draw an object that you would measure to find how much it holds. **6.** Draw an object that you would measure to find its length.

Module 19 • Lesson 1   six hundred forty-nine **649**

DIRECTIONS **7.** Draw an object that you would measure to find its weight.
8. Draw an object that you would measure to find its length.   **9.** Draw an object
that you would measure to find how much it holds.

TEKS Geometry and Measurement—K.7.A
MATHEMATICAL PROCESSES K.1.B

19.1 PROBLEM SOLVING
• Measuring an Object

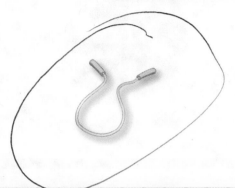

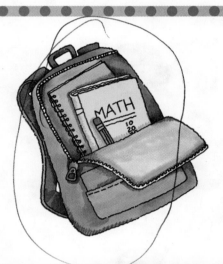

DIRECTIONS **1.** Circle the object you would most likely measure to find how long it is. **2.** Circle the object you would most likely measure to find how much it weighs. **3.** Circle the object you would most likely measure to find how much it holds.

○

○

 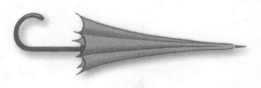

○

DIRECTIONS Choose the correct answer. **4.** Which object would you most likely measure to find how much it weighs? **5.** Which object would you most likely measure to find how long it is? **6.** Which object would you most likely measure to find how much it holds?

TEKS **Geometry and Measurement—K.7.B**

MATHEMATICAL PROCESSES
K.1.D

19.2 HANDS ON
Compare Lengths

Essential Question

How can you compare the lengths of two objects?

Explore Real World

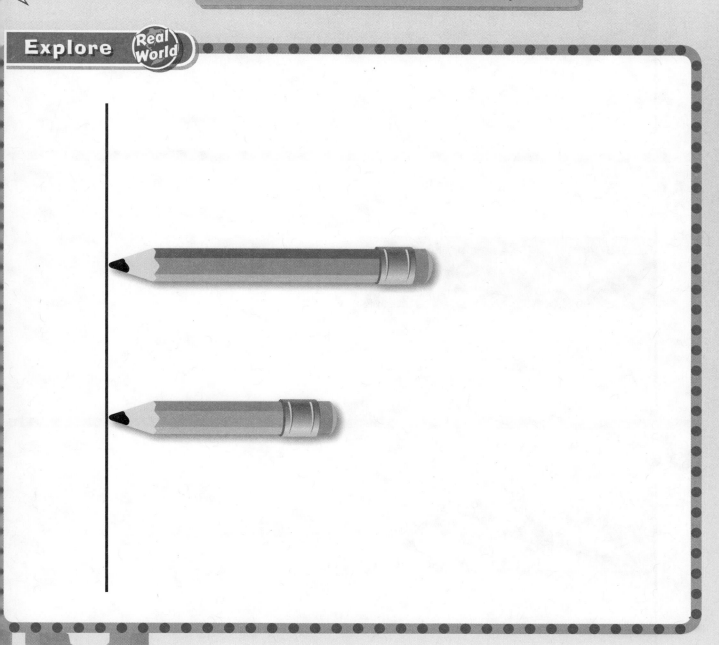

DIRECTIONS Look at the pencils. Compare the lengths of the two pencils. Use the words *longer than*, *shorter than*, or *about the same length* to describe the lengths. Draw around the longer pencil. Draw an X on the shorter pencil.

1 🍎

2 ☀

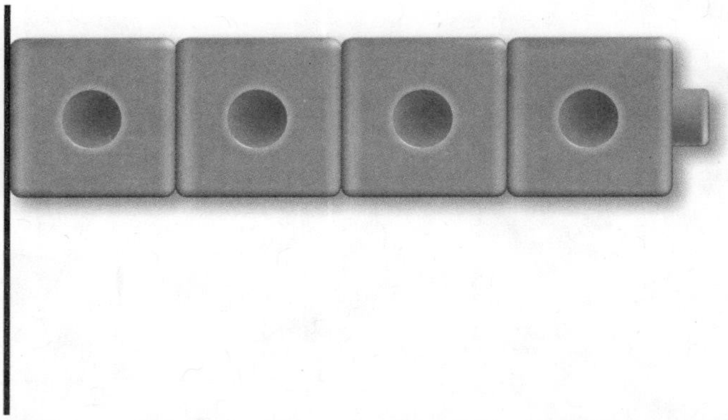

3 ✅

DIRECTIONS **1–3.** Make a cube train that is longer than the cube train shown.
Draw and color the cube train.

654 six hundred fifty-four

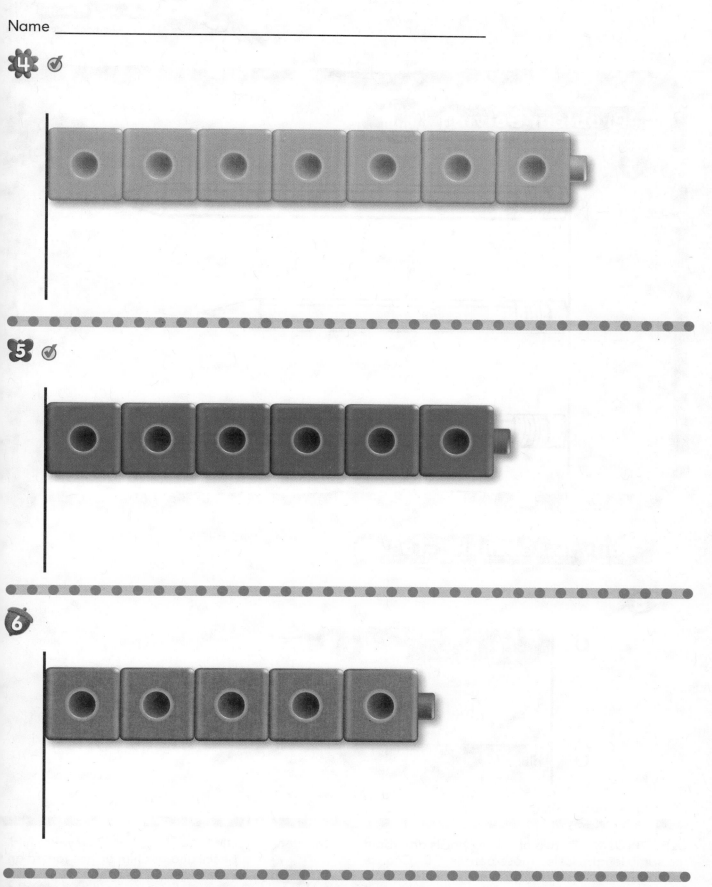

DIRECTIONS **4–6.** Make a cube train that is shorter than the cube train shown. Draw and color the cube train.

Mathematical Processes
Model • Reason • Communicate

Problem Solving Real World

7

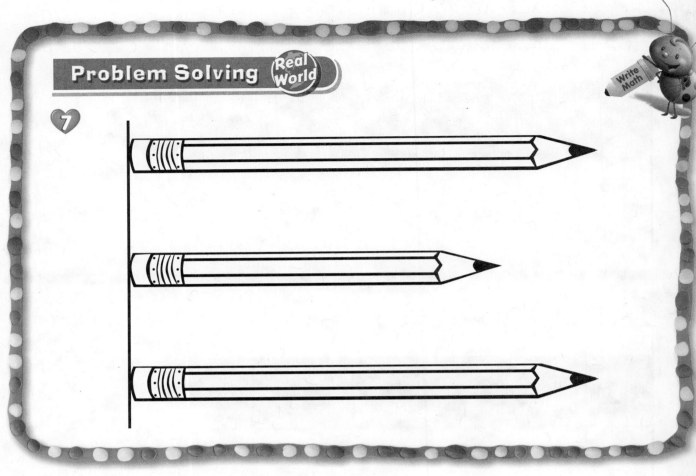

Daily Assessment Task

8

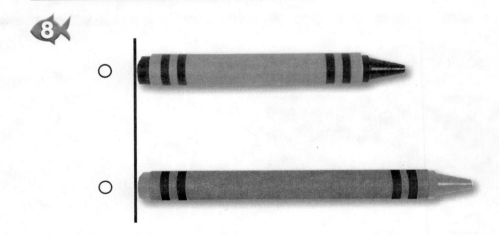

○

○

DIRECTIONS **7.** Two of these pencils are about the same length. Color those pencils. **8.** Choose the correct answer. Which crayon is shorter?

HOME ACTIVITY • Show your child a pencil and ask him or her to find an object that is longer than the pencil. Repeat with an object that is shorter than the pencil and one that is about the same length.

TEKS Geometry and Measurement—K.7.B
MATHEMATICAL PROCESSES K.1.D

Name _____

19.2
HANDS ON

Compare Lengths

1

2

3

DIRECTIONS 1–2. Draw and color a cube train that is longer than the cube train shown. 3. Draw and color a cube train that is shorter than the cube train shown.

Lesson Check

TEXAS Test Prep

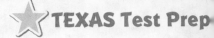

4

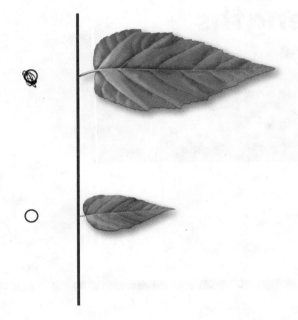

5

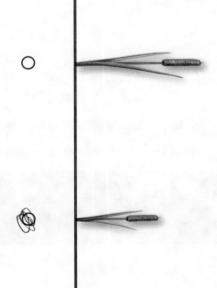

DIRECTIONS Choose the correct answer.
4. Which leaf is longer? **5.** Which cattail is shorter?

TEKS Geometry and Measurement—K.7.B

MATHEMATICAL PROCESSES
K.1.D

19.3
HANDS ON

Compare Heights

? **Essential Question**

How can you compare the heights of two objects?

Explore Real World

DIRECTIONS Look at the chairs. Compare the heights of the two chairs. Use the words *taller than*, *shorter than*, or *about the same height* to describe the heights. Draw around the taller chair. Draw an X on the shorter chair.

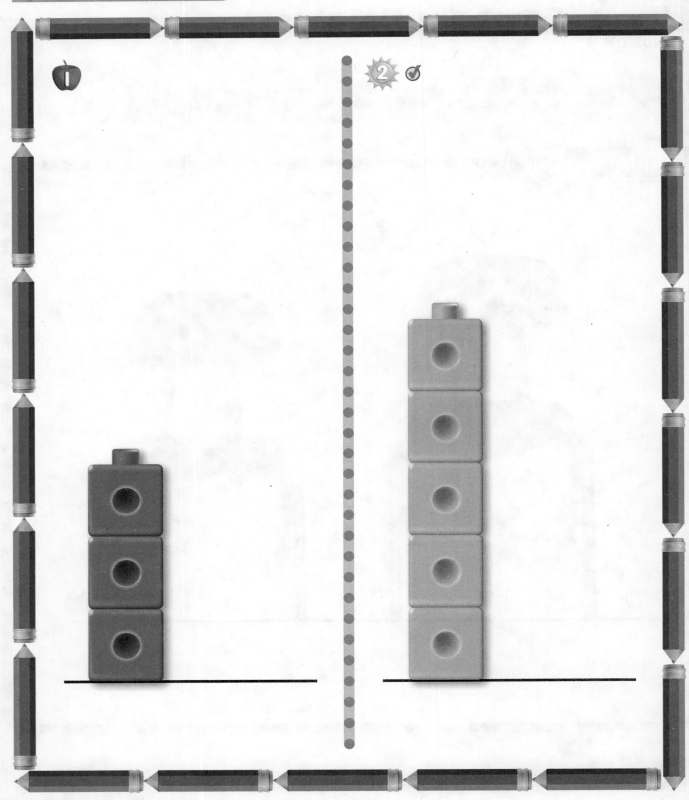

DIRECTIONS **1–2.** Make a cube tower that is taller than the cube tower shown. Draw and color the cube tower.

Name _____

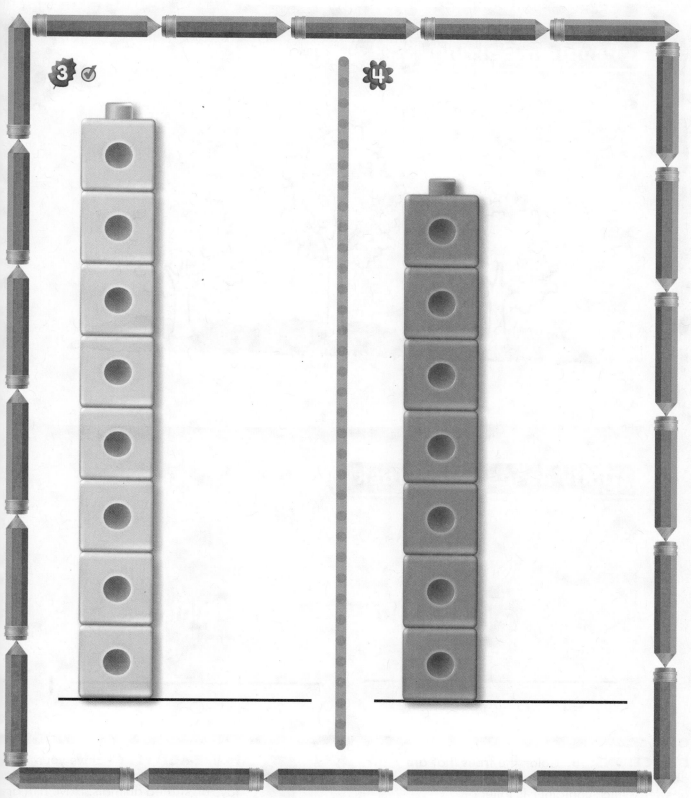

DIRECTIONS **3–4.** Make a cube tower that is shorter than the cube tower shown. Draw and color the cube tower.

Problem Solving Real World

5

Daily Assessment Task

6

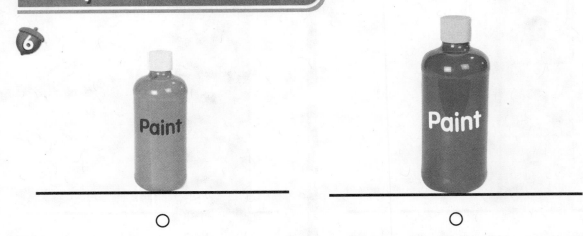

○   ○

DIRECTIONS **5.** Color the trees that are about the same height. **6.** Choose the correct answer. Which container is taller?

HOME ACTIVITY • Have your child find two objects such as plastic toys or stuffed animals. Have him or her place the objects side by side to compare the heights. Ask your child which object is taller and which object is shorter.

Name _____

19.3 Compare Heights
HANDS ON

①

②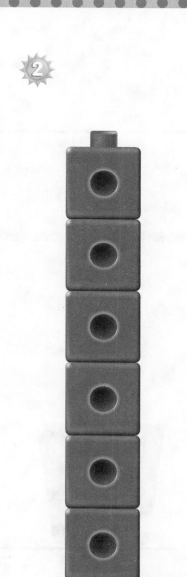

DIRECTIONS 1. Draw and color a cube tower that is taller than the cube tower shown. **2.** Draw and color a cube tower that is shorter than the cube tower shown.

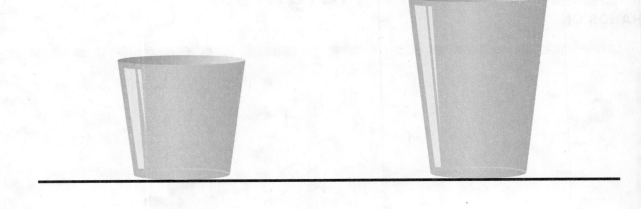

○   ○

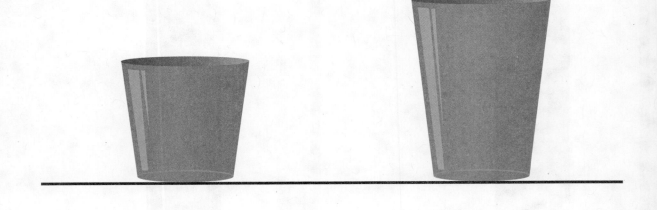

○   ○

DIRECTIONS Choose the correct answer.
3. Which blue glass is taller? **4.** Which red glass is shorter?

Name _____

19.4 Compare Weights

HANDS ON

Essential Question

How can you compare the weights of two objects?

Explore · Real World

DIRECTIONS Look at the picture. Compare the weights of the two objects. Use the words *heavier than*, *lighter than*, or *about the same weight* to describe the weights. Draw a circle around the lighter object. Draw an X on the heavier object.

left   **right**

DIRECTIONS Find the first object in the row, and hold it in your left hand. Find the rest of the objects in the row, and hold each object in your right hand. **1.** Draw a circle around the object that is heavier than the object in your left hand. **2.** Circle the object that is heavier than the object in your left hand. **3–4.** Circle the object that is lighter than the object in your left hand.

5

6

DIRECTIONS Find a book in the classroom. **5.** Find a classroom object that is lighter than the book. Draw it in the work space. **6.** Find a classroom object that is heavier than the book. Draw it in the work space.

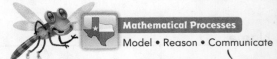
Problem Solving · Real World

7 ♥

Daily Assessment Task

8

○   ○

DIRECTIONS 7. Draw to show what you know about comparing the weights of a piece of paper and another object. Tell a friend about your drawing. **8.** Choose the correct answer. Which pumpkin is lighter?

 HOME ACTIVITY • Have your child compare the weights of two household objects. Then have him or her use the terms *heavier* and *lighter* to describe the weights.

Name _____

19.4
HANDS ON

Compare Weights

DIRECTIONS Find a household object, such as a can of soup. **1.** Find an object that is lighter than the household object. Draw it in the workspace. **2.** Find an object that is heavier than the household object. Draw it in the workspace.

3

○

4

                 ○

5

○

DIRECTIONS Choose the correct answer.
3. Which dog is lighter? **4.** Which duck is heavier?
5. Which object is lighter?

Name _____

 # Module 19 Assessment

Concepts and Skills

 1

○   ○

 2

 3

 4

○   ○

DIRECTIONS   1. Choose the correct answer. Which object would you most likely measure to find out how much it holds? ⬧ TEKS K.7.A **2.** Circle the pencil that is shorter. ⬧ TEKS K.7.B **3.** Circle the cube tower that is taller. ⬧ TEKS K.7.B **4.** Choose the correct answer. Which object is lighter? ⬧ TEKS K.7.B

5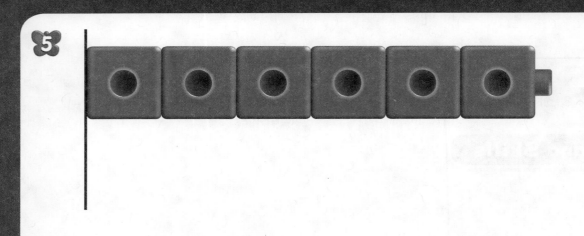

6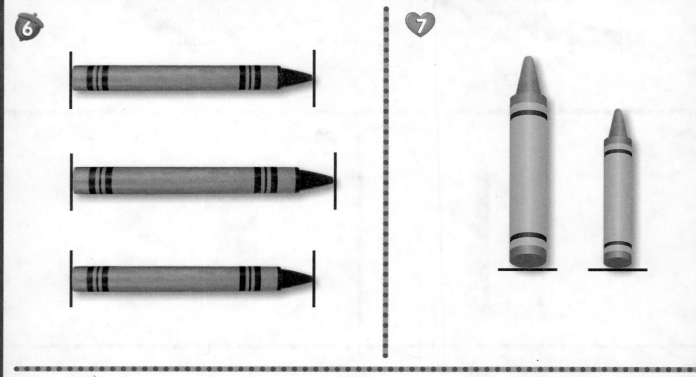

7

8 ⭐ **TEXAS Test Prep**

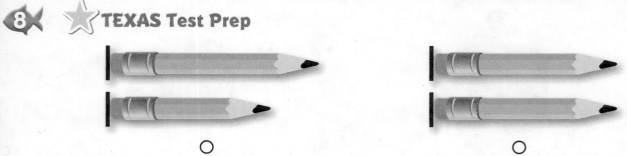

○   ○

DIRECTIONS 5. Make a cube train that is shorter than the one shown. Draw the cube train. ⟍ TEKS K.7.B **6.** Circle the crayons that are about the same length. ⟍ TEKS K.7.B **7.** Circle the crayon that is shorter. ⟍ TEKS K.7.B
8. Choose the correct answer. Which set shows pencils that are about the same length? ⟍ TEKS K.7.B

Name _____

Vocabulary

Concepts and Skills

side

vertex

flat surface

curved surface

DIRECTIONS 1. Use blue to color the sphere. Use green to color the cylinder. Use red to color the cube. Use purple to color the cone. ⬆ TEKS K.6.B **2.** Draw a line from the word *side* to a side of each shape. Draw a line from the word *vertex* to a vertex, or corner, of each shape. ⬆ TEKS K.6.D **3.** Circle the words that describe a cube. ⬆ TEKS K.6.B **4.** I have four square vertices and four straight sides. What am I? Draw the shape. ⬆ TEKS K.6.D

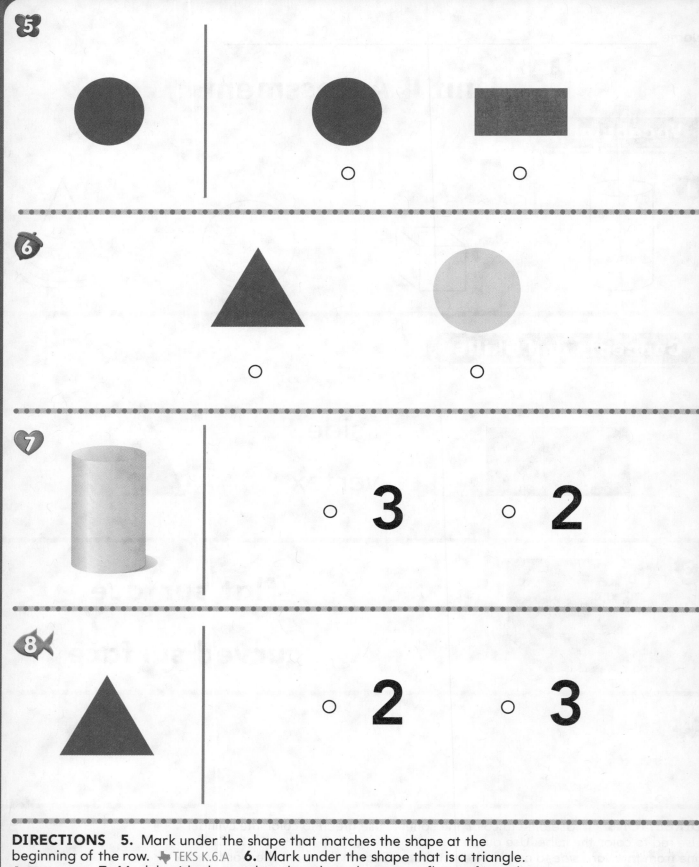

DIRECTIONS **5.** Mark under the shape that matches the shape at the beginning of the row. 🔻TEKS K.6.A **6.** Mark under the shape that is a triangle. 🔻TEKS K.6.A **7.** Mark beside the number that shows how many flat surfaces the cylinder has. TEKS K.6.B **8.** Mark beside the number that shows how many sides the triangle has. 🔻TEKS K.6.D

○   ○

○   ○

○   ○

○   ○

DIRECTIONS **9.** Mark under the shape that is flat. ⬥TEKS K.6.D **10.** Mark under the set that shows a cube and a cylinder. ⬥TEKS K.6.B **11.** Mark under the set that shows a cylinder and a cube. TEKS K.6.B **12.** Mark under the set that shows the green crayon is longer than the blue crayon. ⬥TEKS K.7.B

Performance Task

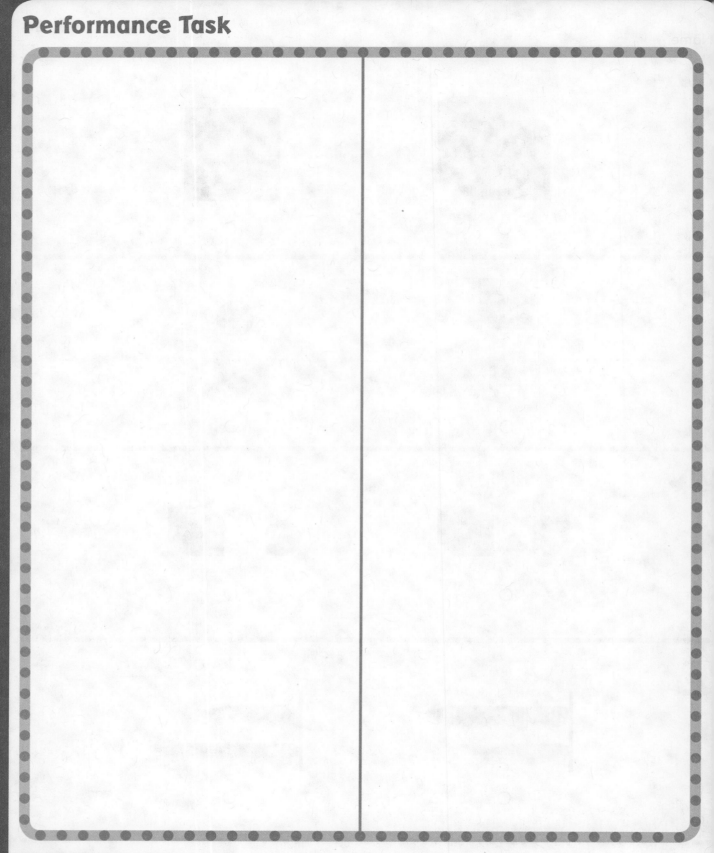

PERFORMANCE TASK   This task will assess the child's understanding of two-dimensional shapes.

Data Analysis

Show What You Know ✓

Name _____

Model More, Model Fewer

 _____   ② _____

_____   _____

Alike and Different

③ _____   _____

_____ sides   _____ vertices

_____ sides   _____ vertices

DIRECTIONS   **1.** Place 4 counters in the five frame. Show one more counter. Write the number. **2.** Place 4 counters in the five frame. Show one fewer counter. Write the number.   **3.** Look at each shape. Write the number of sides and vertices. Tell how the shapes are alike and how they are different.

FAMILY NOTE: This page checks your child's understanding of important skills needed for success in Unit 5.

GO DIGITAL   Assessment Options: Soar to Success Math

Vocabulary Builder

Review Words

blue	square
circle	triangle
rectangle	yellow
red	

Visualize It

Understand Vocabulary

DIRECTIONS **Visualize It** Look at the shapes. Draw a line from the shape on the left to its matching shape on the right.

Understand Vocabulary Draw a triangle. Color it yellow. Draw a square. Color it blue. Draw a circle. Color it red.

• Interactive Student Edition
• Multimedia eGlossary

Pancakes

written by Lucine Perry

illustrated by Bernard Adnet

This Take-Home Book belongs to

_____

Reading and Writing Math

This take-home book will help you review identifying circles, triangles, rectangles, and squares.

MATHEMATICAL PROCESSES K.1.E

Pancake, Pancake! I stir and then I pour.
My family is hungry. I will make some more!
What shape do I make?

Pancake, Pancake!

The batter is very sticky.

I try not to spill any, but that's a little tricky.

What shape do I make?

Pancake, Pancake!
I add some whole wheat.
This makes the cake so tasty to eat.
What shape do I make?

Pancake, Pancake!

Flip when it is golden brown.

We have enough to feed a whole town!

What shape do I make?

Pancakes, Pancakes! I've made so
many now.
Let's make a pancake pattern. I will
show you how.

What shape might come next
in the pattern?

Breakfast is shaping up. It's almost done — hooray!

Can you draw more pancakes with shapes you learned today?

TEKS Data Analysis—
K.8.A *Also K.6.E*

MATHEMATICAL PROCESSES
K.1.E

20.1 Sort by Color and Size

HANDS ON ALGEBRA

Essential Question

How can you sort objects by color or by size into two categories?

Explore

not

DIRECTIONS Choose a color. Use that color crayon to color the pictures of the crayons at the top of the page. Sort a handful of shapes into a set of that color and a set of shapes that are not that color. Draw and color the shapes to show how you sorted.

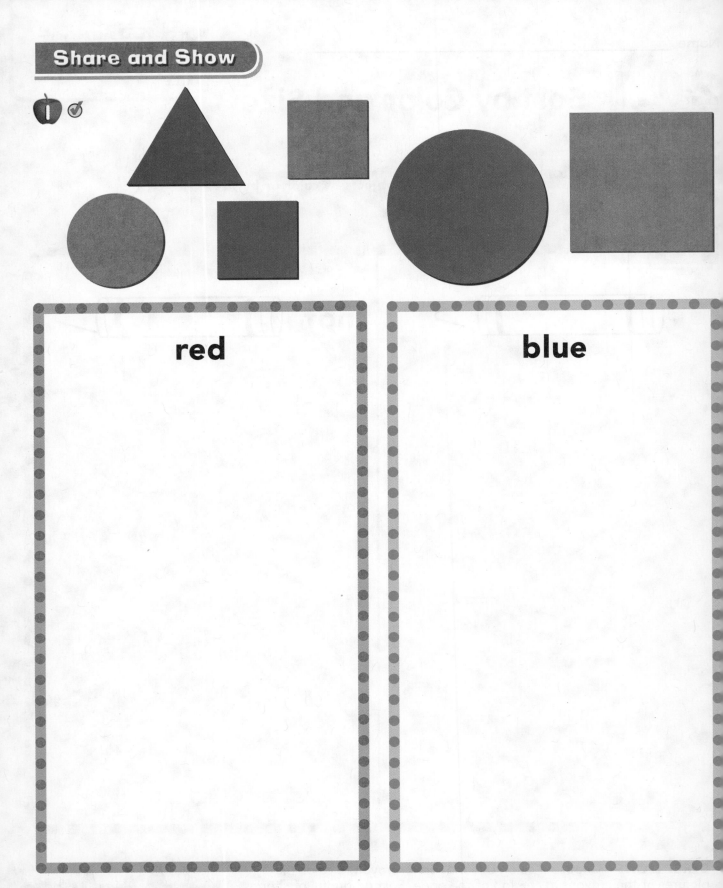

red

blue

DIRECTIONS 1. Use shapes like those shown at the top of the page. Sort the shapes by color. Draw and color the shapes to show how you sorted them.

Name _____

small	big

DIRECTIONS **2.** Use shapes like those shown at the top of the page. Sort the shapes by size. Draw and color the shapes to show how you sorted them.

HOME ACTIVITY • Give your child several objects, such as buttons. Have your child sort the objects into two sets, by color. Then have your child sort the objects again by size.

Problem Solving

3

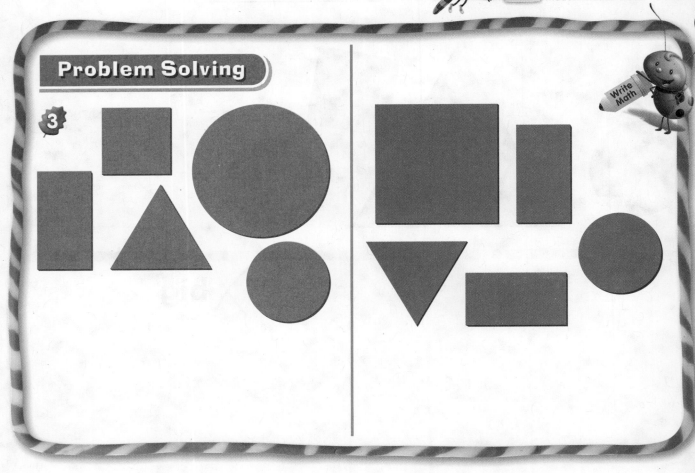

Daily Assessment Task

4

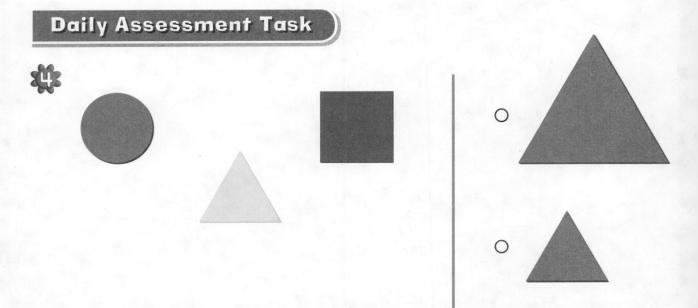

DIRECTIONS **3.** How are these shapes sorted? Draw one more shape in each category. **4.** Choose the correct answer. Which shape belongs in the set?

692 six hundred ninety-two

TEKS Data Analysis—K.8.A
Also K.6.E
MATHEMATICAL PROCESSES K.1.E

Name _____

20.1 Sort by Color and Size

HANDS ON ALGEBRA

blue	yellow

DIRECTIONS **I.** Sort the shapes at the top of the page by color. Draw and color the shapes to show how you sorted them.

Module 20

six hundred ninety-three **693**

2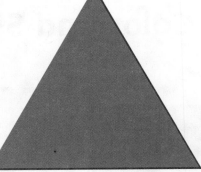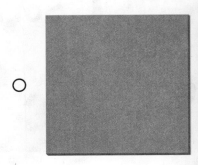

○

○

3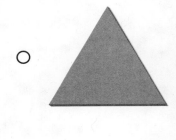

○

○

DIRECTIONS Choose the correct answer.
2–3. Which shape belongs in the set?

Name _____

20.2 Sort into Three Groups

**HANDS ON
ALGEBRA**

Essential Question

How can you sort objects into three categories?

Explore

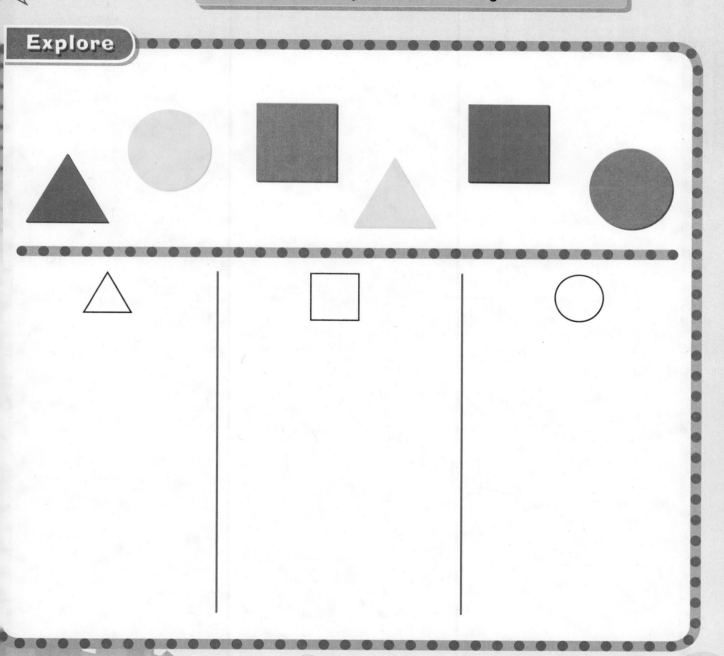

DIRECTIONS Use shapes like those shown at the top of the page. Sort them by shape. Draw and color the shapes to show how you sorted.

Module 20

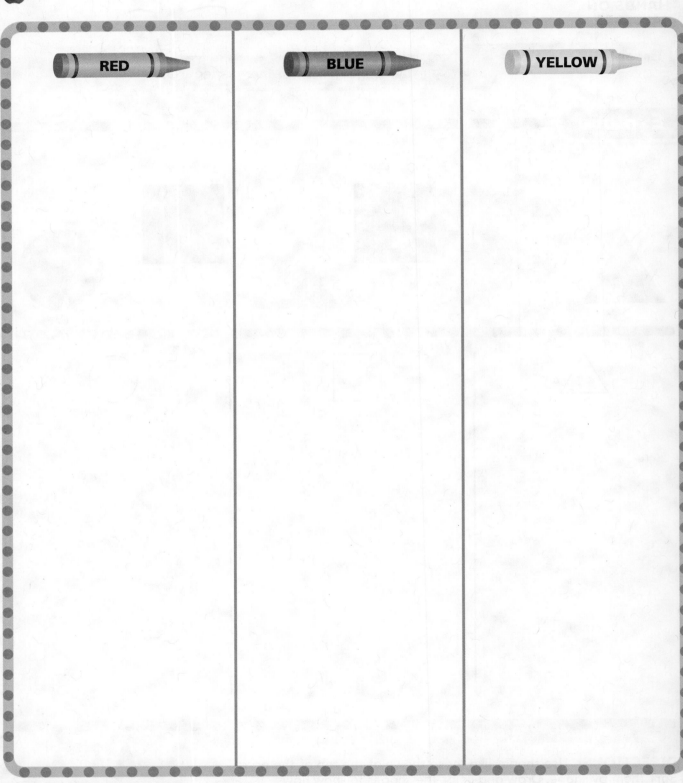

RED   BLUE   YELLOW

DIRECTIONS 1. Take a handful of small shapes. Sort them by color. Draw and color the shapes to show how you sorted.

Name _____

0 sides	3 sides	4 sides

DIRECTIONS **2.** Take a handful of small shapes. Sort them by their number of sides. Draw and color the shapes to show how you sorted.

HOME ACTIVITY • Ask your child to explain how he or she sorted shapes on this page. Draw a square, a circle, or a triangle. Ask your child which category this shape would go in and why.

Problem Solving

3

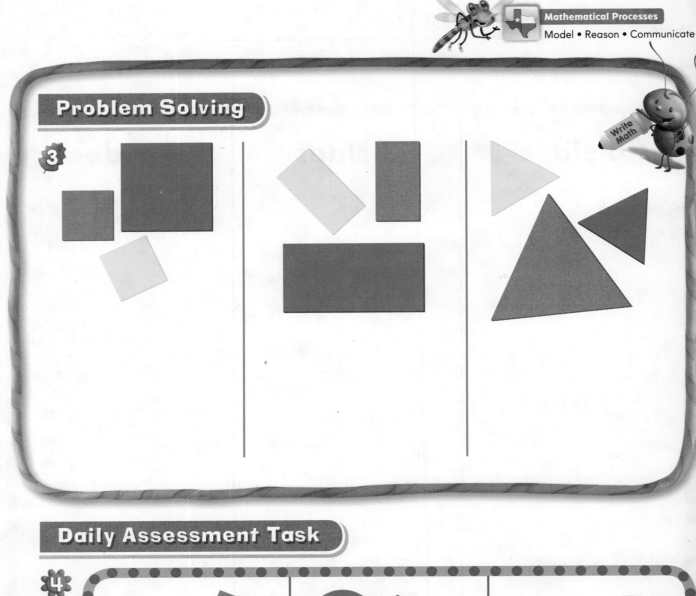

Daily Assessment Task

4

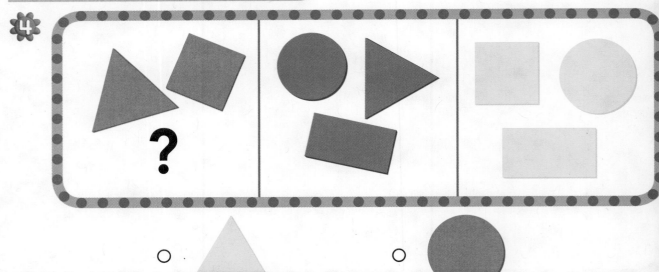

DIRECTIONS **3.** How are the shapes sorted? Draw one more shape in each category. **4.** Choose the correct answer. Look at how the shapes are sorted. Which shape belongs in the first category?

20.2

HANDS ON ALGEBRA

Sort into Three Groups

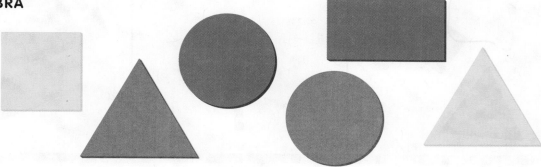

0 sides	3 sides	4 sides

DIRECTIONS **1.** Sort the shapes at the top of the page by their number of sides. Draw and color the shapes to show how you sorted.

?

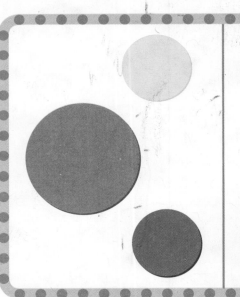

?

DIRECTIONS Choose the correct answer. Look at how the shapes are sorted. **2.** Which shape belongs in the middle category? **3.** Which shape belongs in the last category?

Name _____

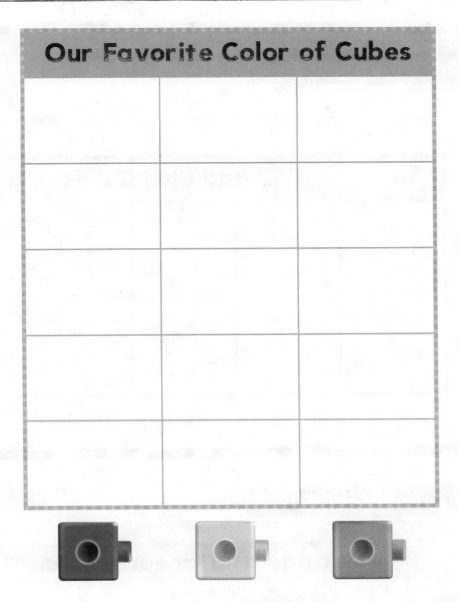

Our Favorite Color of Cubes

_ _ _ _ _ _ _   _ _ _ _ _ _ _   _ _ _ _ _ _ _

_____   _____   _____

DIRECTIONS **4.** Use blue, yellow, and green cubes. Ask 5 classmates to choose their favorite color cube. Place the cubes in the graph. Draw and color the cubes. **5.** Read the graph. Write how many of each color.

HOME ACTIVITY • Have your child tell about the graph that he or she made on this page.

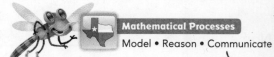

Problem Solving Real World

6

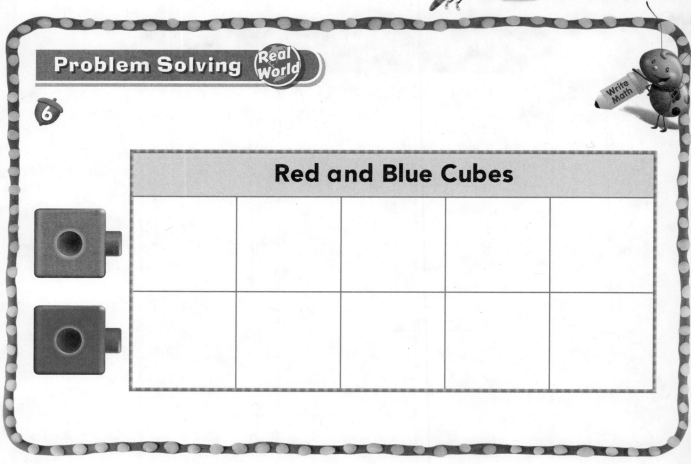

Red and Blue Cubes				

Daily Assessment Task

7

Orange and Green Cubes				

DIRECTIONS **6.** Eli has 3 red cubes. He has two more blue cubes than red cubes. Draw to show the cubes on the graph. **7.** Choose the correct answer. Look at the graph. Are there more orange cubes or more green cubes?

TEKS Data Analysis—K.8.B, K.8.C
Also K.8.A
MATHEMATICAL PROCESSES K.1.D, K.1.E

Name _____

20.3
HANDS ON

Make and Read a Real-Object Graph

1

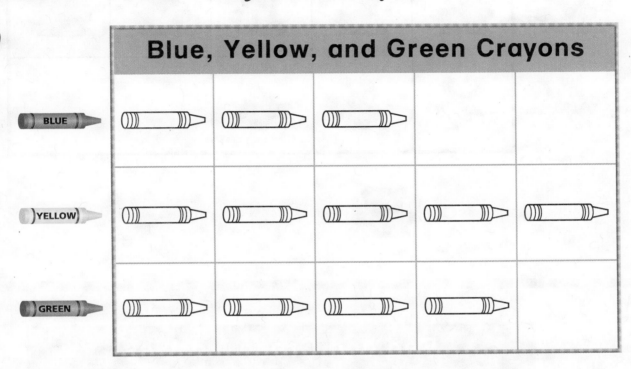

Blue, Yellow, and Green Crayons				
BLUE	🖍	🖍	🖍		
YELLOW	🖍	🖍	🖍	🖍	🖍
GREEN	🖍	🖍	🖍	🖍	

2

BLUE ____   ____   YELLOW ____   ____   GREEN ____   ____

DIRECTIONS Look at the graph. **1.** In the top row, color the crayons blue. In the middle row, color the crayons yellow. In the bottom row, color the crayons green. **2.** Read the graph. Write how many of each color.

3

Blue and Yellow Bears

○   ○

4

Red and Green Marbles

○   ○

DIRECTIONS Choose the correct answer.
3. Are there more yellow bears or more blue bears? **4.** Are there more red marbles or more green marbles?

HANDS ON

Make and Read a Picture Graph

TEKS Data Analysis—
K.8.B, K.8.C *Also K.8.A*
MATHEMATICAL PROCESSES
K.1.D, K.1.E

Essential Question How can you use a picture graph to show objects sorted into categories?

Explore

Red and Yellow Cubes

Red and Yellow Cubes

DIRECTIONS Look at the graph at the top of the page. Listen to the problem. Use cubes to show the problem. Look at the graph at the bottom of the page. Draw circles to show the cubes at the top of the page.

Blue, Green, and Red Cubes

Blue and Green Cubes

DIRECTIONS **1.** Use the cubes shown at the top of the page. Sort the cubes and move them to the graph. Draw circles to show the cubes. **2.** Read the graph. Which color has fewer cubes? Circle the cube below the graph.

708 seven hundred eight

Name _____

3

Animals

4

_____   _____   _____
- - - - -   - - - - -   - - - - -
_____   _____   _____

DIRECTIONS 3. Look at the picture. How many of each animal are there? Draw circles in the graph to show the number of each animal. **4.** Write how many of each animal.

HOME ACTIVITY • Have your child draw another rabbit in the picture at the top of the page. Ask your child to change the graph to match the picture and explain why the graph changed.

Problem Solving

5

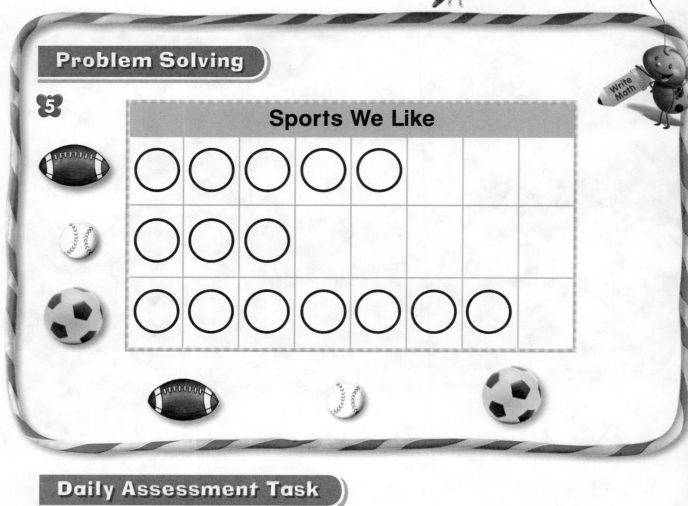

Sports We Like

Daily Assessment Task

6

Fruit We Like

○ **4**

○ **5**

DIRECTIONS **5.** Read the picture graph. Circle the ball to show the sport that the most children like. **6.** Choose the correct answer. How many children like apples?

Homework and Practice

Name _____

20.4
HANDS ON

Make and Read a Picture Graph

Sea Animals				

 _____
 - - - - - - - -

 _____
- - - - - - - -

 _____
- - - - - - - -

DIRECTIONS **1.** Look at the fish tank. How many of each sea animal are there? Draw circles in the graph to show the number of each sea animal. **2.** Write the number of each sea animal.

3

Cars We Like					
O	O	O			
O	O	O	O	O	

○ **3**   ○ **5**

4

Favorite Forest Animal					
O	O	O	O	O	O
O	O	O	O		

○ **6**   ○ **4**

DIRECTIONS Choose the correct answer.
3. How many children like yellow cars?
4. How many children like rabbits?

20.5 PROBLEM SOLVING • Collect Data and Create a Graph

TEKS **Data Analysis—**
K.8.C *Also K.8.A, K.8.B*
MATHEMATICAL PROCESSES
K.1.B, K.1.D, K.1.E

Essential Question

How can you collect data and use that data to create a graph?

Unlock the Problem (Real World)

Kinds of Shoes				

 _____

 _ _ _ _ _ _ _ _

DIRECTIONS Ask five of your classmates whether their shoes have laces or no laces. Draw circles on the picture graph to show their answers. Write how many of each kind of shoe.

Try Another Problem

1

Favorite Fruit

2

_____   _____   _____

- - - - - - - - -   - - - - - - - - -   - - - - - - - - -

_____   _____   _____

3

DIRECTIONS **1.** Ask five of your classmates whether they like bananas, apples, or oranges best. Draw circles on the picture graph to show their answers. **2.** Write how many children like each kind of fruit. **3.** Circle the fruit that more children like.

Name _____

 4

How We Get to School					

5

 _____  _____  _____

 6

DIRECTIONS   4. Ask five classmates how they got to school in the morning. Draw circles on the picture graph to show their answers.   **5.** Write the number of children.   **6.** Circle the picture that shows how fewer children got to school.

 HOME ACTIVITY • Ask your child to explain how he or she completed the graph. Then ask a question such as: Did more children walk or take the bus to school?

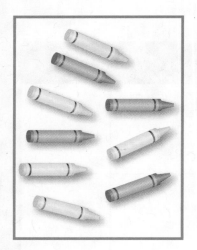

Red and Yellow Crayons					
○	○	○	○		

○ **5**   ○ **4**

Cars and Trucks					
○	○	○			

○ **2**   ○ **3**

DIRECTIONS Choose the correct answer. **7.** Allie sorts the crayons and makes a graph. How many circles will Allie draw in the second row of the graph? **8.** David sorts his toys and makes a graph. How many circles will he draw in the second row of the graph?

Name _____

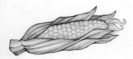

20.5 PROBLEM SOLVING • Collect
Data and Create a Graph

Kinds of Vegetables					

   _____      _____

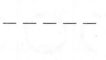

DIRECTIONS **I.** Ask five friends or family members if they like corn or potatoes. Draw circles on the picture graph to show their answers. **2.** Write how many people like each vegetable. **3.** Circle the vegetable that more people like.

 4

 6

Stickers

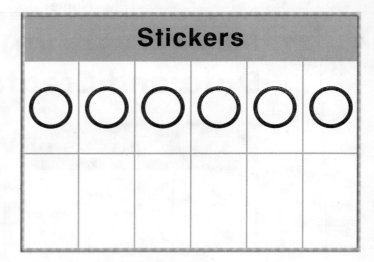

 5

5

 3

Purple and Green Marbles

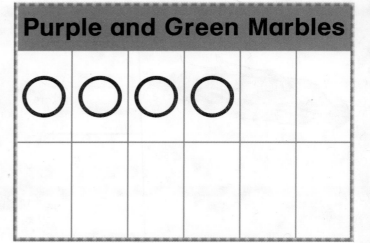

 4

DIRECTIONS Choose the correct answer.
4. Jen sorts the stickers and makes a graph. How many circles will Jen draw in the second row of the graph? **5.** Brad sorts the marbles and makes a graph. How many circles will he draw in the second row of the graph?

Unit 5 Assessment

Vocabulary

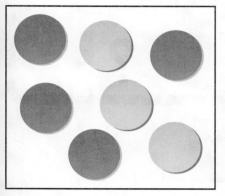

Red and Yellow Counters			
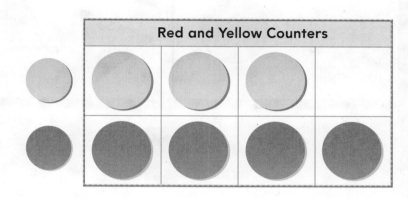

Concepts and Skills

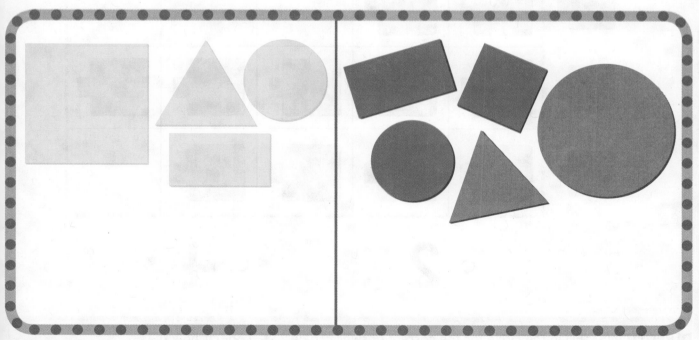

DIRECTIONS **1.** Circle the graph. ★ TEKS K.8.B **2.** How are the shapes sorted?
Draw one more shape in each category. ★ TEKS K.8.A

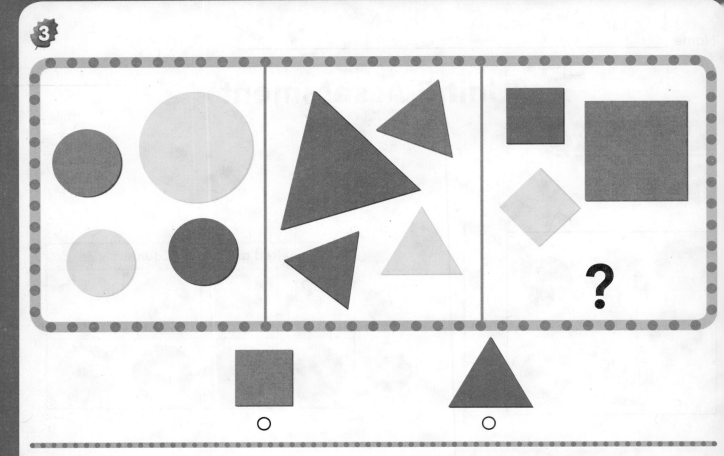

○   ○

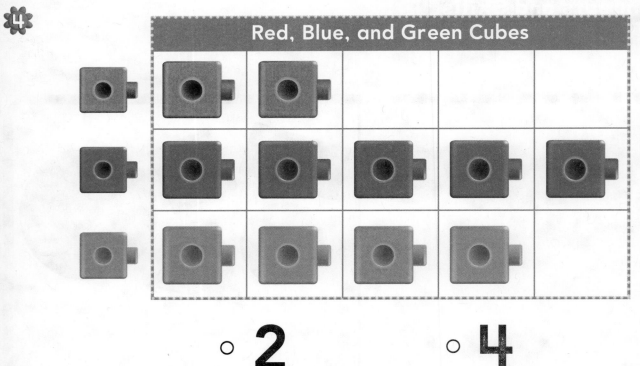

Red, Blue, and Green Cubes

○ **2**   ○ **4**

DIRECTIONS Fill in the circle for the correct answer choice. **3.** Look at how the shapes are sorted. Which shape belongs in the last category? ◆ TEKS K.8.A **4.** Look at the graph. How many green cubes are there? ◆ TEKS K.8.C

5

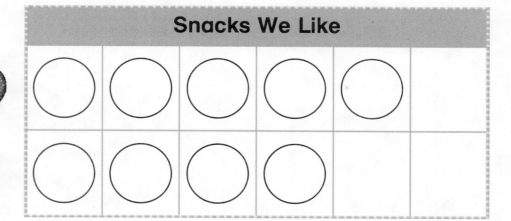

Snacks We Like

○ **5**

○ **6**

6

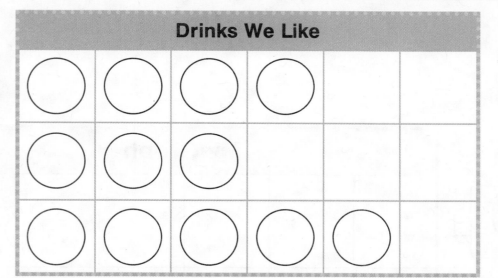

Drinks We Like

○ **4**

○ **5**

7

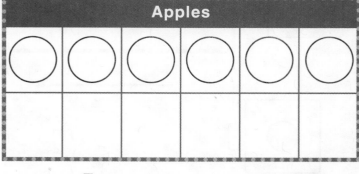

Apples

○ **6**   ○ **4**

DIRECTIONS 5. Look at the picture graph. How many children like pretzels? ⬥ TEKS K.8.C
6. Look at the picture graph. How many children like water? ⬥ TEKS K.8.C **7.** Callie sorts the
apples and makes a graph. How many circles will she draw in the bottom row? ⬥ TEKS K.8.B

Performance Task

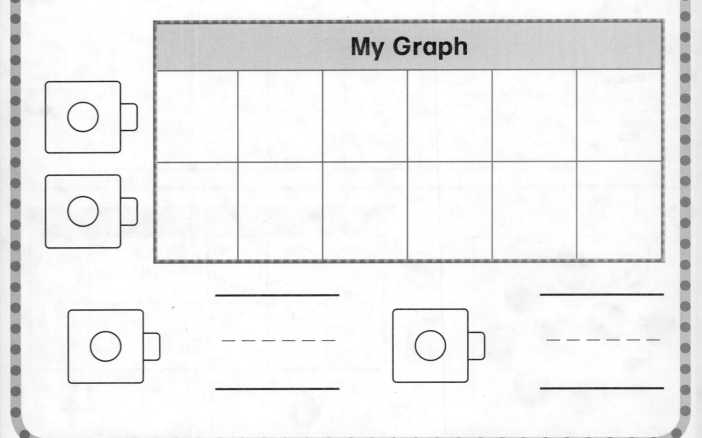

My Graph

PERFORMANCE TASK   This task will assess the child's understanding of sorting and graphing.

Personal Financial Literacy

Show What You Know ✓

Name _____

Sort by Shape

Make a Concrete Graph

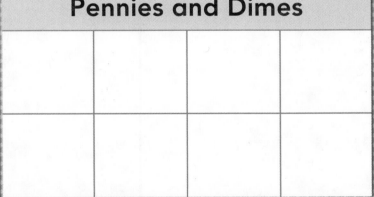

Pennies and Dimes

DIRECTIONS **1.** Circle the triangles.
2. Place coins on the pictured coins. Sort the coins and move them to the graph. Draw the coins.

 FAMILY NOTE: This page checks your child's understanding of important skills needed for success in Unit 6.

Visualize It

Understand Vocabulary

DIRECTIONS **Visualize It** Look at the coins. Draw a line from the coin on the left to its matching coin on the right.

Understand Vocabulary Place coins on the pictured coins above. Sort the coins into two groups. Draw the coins you sorted. Explain how you sorted the coins.

Summer Fun

written by Tim Johnson

illustrated by Promotion Studios

This Take-Home Book belongs to

Joordan

Can you find these four shapes on each page of the story?

Reading and Writing Math

This take-home book will help you review identifying cylinders, cones, and spheres.

MATHEMATICAL PROCESSES K.1.A, K.1.D

"Yippee!" the mice shout.
"Our yard work's all done!
Let's go to the beach
For some good summer fun."

The mice pack a picnic,
Some sunscreen and chairs,
Speed off in their car,
Leave behind all their cares.

The day was so pretty,
So sunny and warm.
No clouds in the sky,
And no sign of a storm.

When at last to the beach
The mice did arrive,
They said to each other,
"What a happy, fun drive!"

Find the shapes one more time!
Then circle your favorite ice pop shape!

Write about the Math

Vocabulary Review
work

DIRECTIONS Look at the picture. Draw pictures that show someone doing some kind of work. Tell a friend about the work being done in your pictures.

Who Does Work?

2

DIRECTIONS **1–2.** Look at the pictures. Circle the mice doing work.

Name _____

21.1 Earn Money

Essential Question How do you identify ways that income can be earned?

Explore Real World

_____   _____

_ _ _ _ _ _ _ _   _ _ _ _ _ _ _ _

_____   _____

DIRECTIONS Sam and Ellie are earning money by selling lemonade. Look at the sign on the lemonade stand. Write the number of pennies they will earn if someone buys a small lemonade. Write the number of pennies they will earn if someone buys a large lemonade.

1

2 ✓

DIRECTIONS 1–2. Circle the picture of a child working to earn income. Put an X on the picture that shows a child playing.

736 seven hundred thirty-six

3

DIRECTIONS **3.** Cut out pictures of people doing activities at work and play. Place and glue the pictures of people working to earn money in the first column. Place and glue the pictures of people doing an activity in their free time in the second column.

HOME ACTIVITY • Talk about people in your child's daily life who do jobs to earn money, such as a crossing guard, a bus driver, or a fire fighter.

Problem Solving

4

20

Daily Assessment Task

5

○   ○

DIRECTIONS 4. Jasmine walks a dog once a day. Each day she earns 10 pennies. How many pennies does she earn in two days? Write the number. **5.** Choose the correct answer. Which picture shows a way to earn money?

TEKS Personal Financial Literacy—K.9.A
Also K.8.A
MATHEMATICAL PROCESSES K.1.A, K.1.D

Name _____

21.1 Earn Money

 1

 2

DIRECTIONS   1–2. Circle the picture of a child working to earn income. Put an X on the picture that shows a child playing.

3

4

DIRECTIONS Choose the correct answer.
3–4. Which picture shows a way to earn money?

Name _____

21.2   Receive Money

TEKS Personal Financial
Literacy—K.9.B
Also K.2.G, K.8.A
MATHEMATICAL PROCESSES
K.1.A, K.1.D

Essential Question   What is the difference between earning money and receiving money as a gift?

Explore Real World

DIRECTIONS Sarah cleans her sister's room and earns 10 pennies. Alex receives 10 pennies from his grandfather as a gift. How many pennies did Sarah earn? Write the number. How many pennies did Alex receive? Write the number. Circle the picture of the child who earned money.

Apples for Sale

DIRECTIONS **1–2.** Circle the picture that shows a child earning money. Put an X on the picture that shows a child receiving money as a gift.

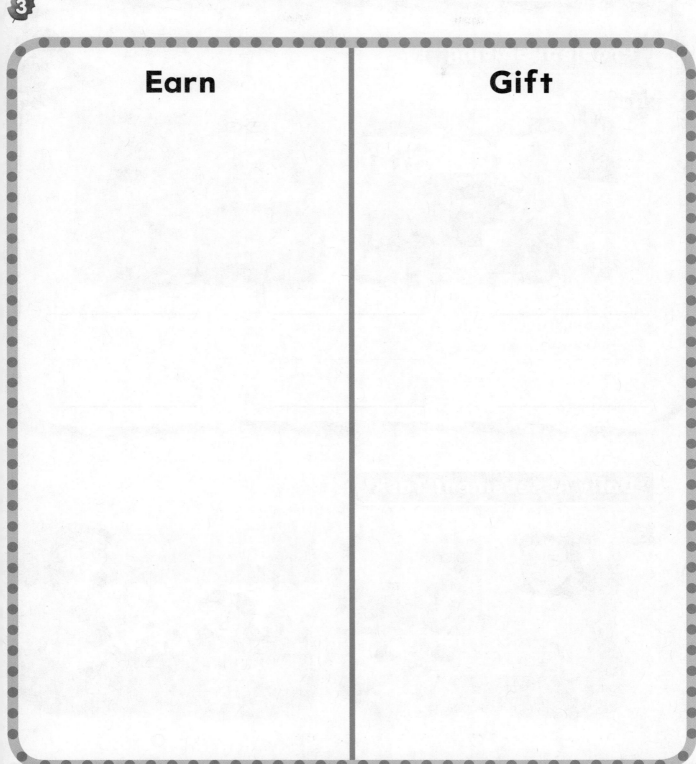

Earn

Gift

HOME ACTIVITY • Talk about ways your child could earn money as income such as doing chores around the home or for neighbors.

Problem Solving

4

_____ _____ _____

Daily Assessment Task

5

⃝   ⃝

DIRECTIONS 4. Mikah earns 10 pennies from a neighbor for raking leaves. Write the number. He receives 5 pennies from his grandmother as a gift. Write the number. How many pennies did Mikah receive in all? Write the number. **5.** Choose the correct answer. Aunt Olivia gives Elena money as a gift. Which picture shows how Elena gets the money?

TEKS Personal Financial Literacy—K.9.B
Also K.2.G, K.8.A
MATHEMATICAL PROCESSES K.1.A, K.1.D

Name _____

21.2 Receive Money

DIRECTIONS **1–2.** Circle the picture that shows a child earning money. Put an X on the picture that shows a child receiving money as a gift.

Module 21

seven hundred forty-five **745**

 3

○   ○

 4

○   ○

DIRECTIONS Choose the correct answer.
3. Uncle John gives David money he has earned.
Which picture shows how David earns the money?
4. Grandmother gives Ella money as a gift. Which
picture shows how Ella gets the money?

21.3 Use Money for Wants and Needs

TEKS Personal Financial Literacy—K.9.D
Also K.8.A
MATHEMATICAL PROCESSES
K.1.A, K.1.D

Essential Question

What is the difference between a want and a need?

Explore Real World

DIRECTIONS Maeve is packing for a weekend trip to her grandparents' house. She has packed some things she needs to take and some things she wants to take. Circle the items that Maeve needs. Place an X on the items that she wants.

1

2 ✓

DIRECTIONS **1.** Circle the picture that shows a want. **2.** Circle the picture that shows a need.

DIRECTIONS **3.** Anna earned money helping her mom rake leaves. She uses the money she earned to buy what she needs for school. Circle the picture that shows items that Anna buys. **4.** Mr. Jacobs goes to the market. Since he has everything he needs, he buys something he wants. Circle the picture that shows what Mr. Jacobs buys.

HOME ACTIVITY • Sort items such as groceries and toys with your child to determine which objects are needs and which are wants.

Mathematical Processes
Model • Reason • Communicate

Problem Solving

5

Daily Assessment Task

6

○   ○

DIRECTIONS **5.** Molly uses her allowance money to buy something she needs. Circle the picture that shows what Molly buys. **6.** Choose the correct answer. Which picture shows a need?

TEKS Personal Financial Literacy—K.9.D
Also K.8.A
MATHEMATICAL PROCESSES K.1.A, K.1.D

Name _____

21.3 Use Money for Wants and Needs

DIRECTIONS **1.** Circle the picture that shows a need. **2.** Circle the picture that shows a want.

 3

◯

 **4**

◯

DIRECTIONS Choose the correct answer.
3. Which picture shows a want? **4.** Which picture shows a need?

Name _____

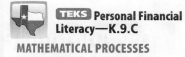
21.4

PROBLEM SOLVING • Connect
Skills to a Job

Essential Question

How do you identify what skills are needed for a job?

Unlock the Problem Real World

DIRECTIONS Circle the person who needs to know how to: measure someone's temperature in blue; safely put out a fire in red; use a wrench properly in green.

Try Another Problem

$2.01

DIRECTIONS **I.** Circle the person who needs to know how to: measure for a recipe in blue; follow directions on a map in green; count money in red; read music in yellow.

Name _____

DIRECTIONS 2. Circle the person who needs to know how to: listen to an animal's heartbeat in blue; use a food scale in green; measure rainfall in red; measure distance in yellow.

HOME ACTIVITY • Ask your child what job he or she might like to do when he or she grows up. Discuss the tools and skills that are needed for that job.

Module 21 • Lesson 4

seven hundred fifty-five **755**

3

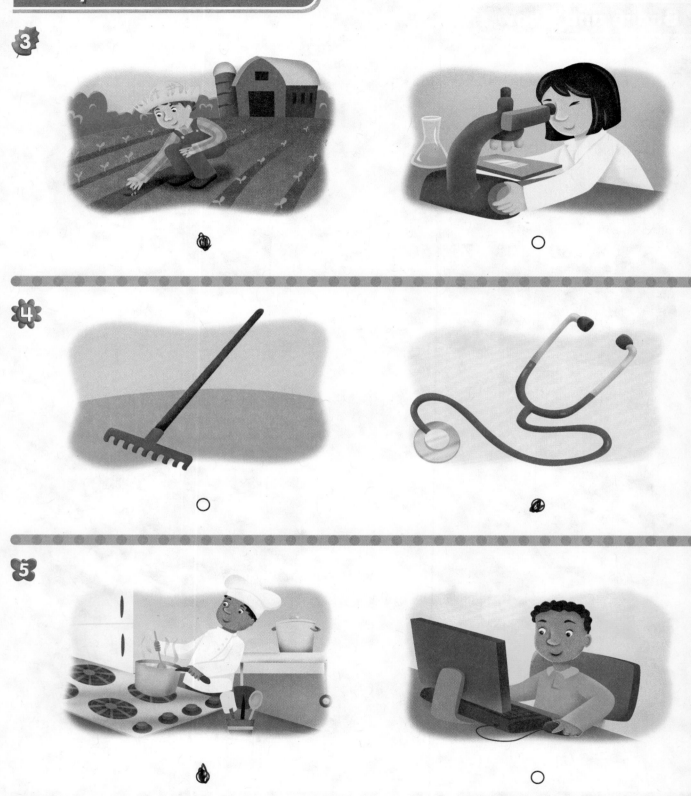

4

5

DIRECTIONS Choose the correct answer. **3.** For which job do you need to know how to plant seeds? **4.** Which does a doctor need to know how to use at work? **5.** Raj is a great cook. Which picture shows him using his skill?

756 seven hundred fifty-six

TEKS Personal Financial Literacy—K.9.C
MATHEMATICAL PROCESSES K.1.A, K.1.B, K.1.D

Name _____

21.4 PROBLEM SOLVING
• Connect Skills to a Job

DIRECTIONS I. Circle the person who needs to know how to: create a picture in blue; measure length in green; safely drive a bus in red; fix an engine in yellow.

○   ○

○   ○

○   ○

DIRECTIONS Choose the correct answer.
2. Mr. Murphy needs to know how to safely put out a fire. Which picture shows Mr. Murphy? **3.** Nancy needs to know how to use a camera. Which picture shows Nancy? **4.** Mr. Romero needs to know how to teach children to read. Which picture shows Mr. Romero at work?

Name _____

 # Unit 6 Assessment

Vocabulary

Concepts and Skills

DIRECTIONS **1.** Draw a line to connect the money to a way to earn income. ⬇ TEKS K.9.A
2–3. Circle the picture that shows a child earning money. ⬇ TEKS K.9.A

4

○   ○

5

○   ○

6

○   ○

DIRECTIONS Choose the correct answer. **4.** Which picture shows money earned? ⬙TEKS K.9.B **5.** Rachel's mom gives her money as a gift. Which picture shows how Rachel gets the money? ⬙TEKS K.9.B **6.** Tamara is a great cook. Which picture shows her using her skill? ⬙TEKS K.9.C

7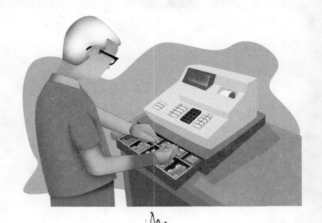

8

○

9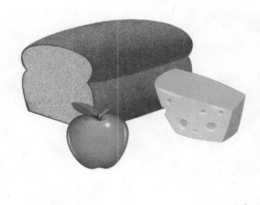

○ ○

DIRECTIONS Choose the correct answer. **7.** Which picture shows a person who needs to know how to count money? ☜ TEKS K.9.C **8.** Which picture shows a want? ☜ TEKS K.9.D **9.** John goes to the store with his mom. He buys what he needs. Which picture shows what John and his mom buy? ☜ TEKS K.9.D

Performance Task

PERFORMANCE TASK This task will assess the child's understanding of earning money.

762 seven hundred sixty-two

Picture Glossary

add sumar

$$3 + 2 = 5$$

alike igual

and y

 and

$$2 + 2$$

big grande

big

capacity capacidad

Capacity is how much
something can hold.

category categoría

fruits

toys

circle círculo

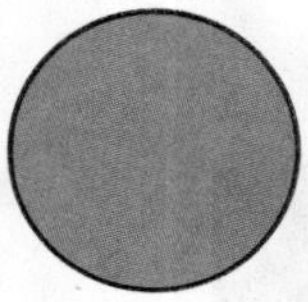

classify clasificar

apples

not apples

color color

red
rojo

blue
azul

yellow
amarillo

green
verde

orange
anaranjado

compare comparar

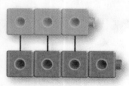

cone cono

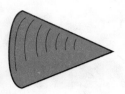

corner esquina

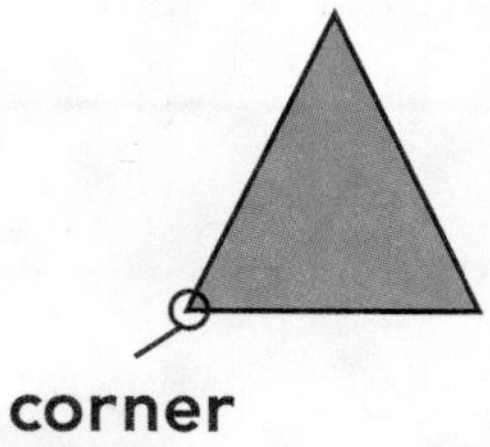

corner

count backward contar hacia atrás

5, 4, 3, 2, 1

count forward contar hacia adelante

1, 2, 3, 4, 5

cube cubo

curved curva

The edge of a circle is
curved.

curved surface
superficie curva

Some solids have
a **curved surface**.

cylinder cilindro

different diferente

dime moneda de diez
centavos

earn ganar

You **earn** income when
you work.

eight ocho

eighteen dieciocho

eleven once

fewer menos

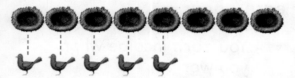

fewer birds

fifteen quince

fifty cincuenta

1	2	3	4	5	6	7	8	9	10
11	12	13	14	15	16	17	18	19	20
21	22	23	24	25	26	27	28	29	30
31	32	33	34	35	36	37	38	39	40
41	42	43	44	45	46	47	48	49	50

five cinco

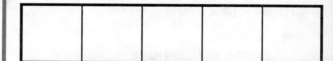

five frame cuadro de cinco

flat plano

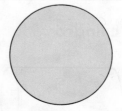

A circle is a **flat** shape.

flat surface superficie plana

Some solids have a
flat surface.

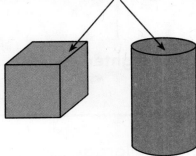

graph gráfica

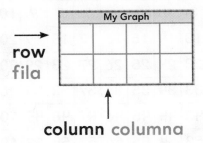

row
fila

column columna

four cuatro

greater mayor

9 is **greater** than 6

6

9

fourteen catorce

heavier más pesado

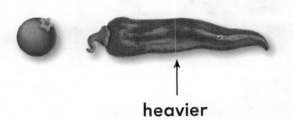

heavier

hundred chart tabla con los números hasta el 100

1	2	3	4	5	6	7	8	9	10
11	12	13	14	15	16	17	18	19	20
21	22	23	24	25	26	27	28	29	30
31	32	33	34	35	36	37	38	39	40
41	42	43	44	45	46	47	48	49	50
51	52	53	54	55	56	57	58	59	60
61	62	63	64	65	66	67	68	69	70
71	72	73	74	75	76	77	78	79	80
81	82	83	84	85	86	87	88	89	90
91	92	93	94	95	96	97	98	99	100

is equal to es igual a

$3 + 2 = 5$

$3 + 2$ **is equal to** 5

less menor/menos

9 **is less** than 11

9

11

lighter más liviano

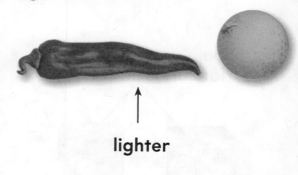

lighter

longer más largo

longer

match emparejar

minus – menos

$4 - 3 = 1$

4 **minus** 3 is equal to 1

---

more más

more leaves

---

nickel moneda de cinco centavas

nine nueve

---

nineteen diecinueve

---

one uno

one hundred cien

1	2	3	4	5	6	7	8	9	10
11	12	13	14	15	16	17	18	19	20
21	22	23	24	25	26	27	28	29	30
31	32	33	34	35	36	37	38	39	40
41	42	43	44	45	46	47	48	49	50
51	52	53	54	55	56	57	58	59	60
61	62	63	64	65	66	67	68	69	70
71	72	73	74	75	76	77	78	79	80
81	82	83	84	85	86	87	88	89	90
91	92	93	94	95	96	97	98	99	100

order orden

The numbers are in **order** from 1 to 5.

1, 2, 3, 4, 5

pairs pares

number **pairs** for 3

3 and 0
2 and 1
1 and 2
0 and 3

penny moneda de un centavo

picture graph gráfica de dibujos

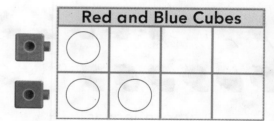

Red and Blue Cubes

plus + más

2 **plus** 1 is equal to 3
2 + 1 = 3

quarter moneda de veinticinco centavos

real-object graph gráfica de objetos reales

rectangle rectángulo

same height de la misma altura

same length del mismo largo

same number el mismo número

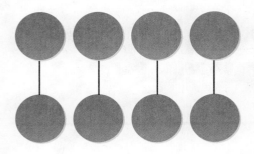

same weight del mismo peso

seven siete

seventeen diecisiete

shape forma

shorter más corto

shorter

side lado

side

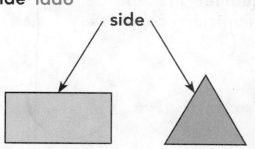

sides of equal length lados del mismo largo

six seis

sixteen dieciséis

size tamaño

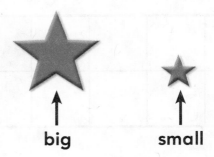

↑ big   ↑ small

small pequeño

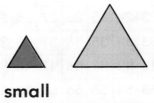

small

solid sólido

solid

A **cylinder** is a solid shape.

sort clasificar

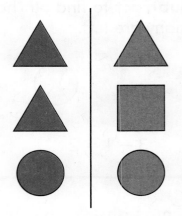

sphere esfera

square cuadrado

subtract restar

Subtract to find out how many are left.

$$3 - 1 = 2$$

---

taller más alto

taller

---

ten diez

ten frame cuadro de diez

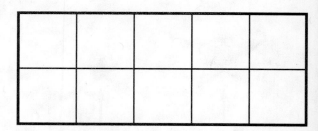

---

tens decenas

1	2	3	4	5	6	7	8	9	10
11	12	13	14	15	16	17	18	19	20
21	22	23	24	25	26	27	28	29	30
31	32	33	34	35	36	37	38	39	40
41	42	43	44	45	46	47	48	49	50
51	52	53	54	55	56	57	58	59	60
61	62	63	64	65	66	67	68	69	70
71	72	73	74	75	76	77	78	79	80
81	82	83	84	85	86	87	88	89	90
91	92	93	94	95	96	97	98	99	100

tens

---

thirteen trece

three tres

---

three-dimensional shapes
figuras tridimensionales

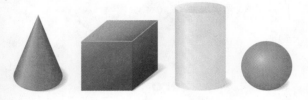

---

triangle triángulo

---

twelve doce

twenty veinte

---

two dos

---

two-dimensional shapes
figuras bidimensionales

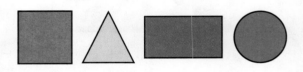

---

vertex vértice

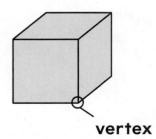

vertex

vertices vértices

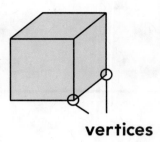

vertices

weight peso

zero, none cero, ninguno

zero fish